Elite • 135

German Air Forces
1914–18

Ian Sumner • Illustrated by Graham Sumner

Consultant editor Martin Windrow

First published in Great Britain in 2005 by Osprey Publishing,
Midland House, West Way, Botley, Oxford OX2 0PH, UK
443 Park Avenue South, New York, NY 10016, USA
Email: info@ospreypublishing.com

ISBN 1 84176 924 X

Design: Ken Vail Graphic Design, Cambridge, UK (kvgd.com)
Index by Alison Worthington
Originated by PPS Grasmere Ltd, Leeds, UK
Printed in China through World Print Ltd.

05 06 07 08 09   10 9 8 7 6 5 4 3 2 1

A CIP catalogue record for this book is available from the British Library

FOR A CATALOGUE OF ALL BOOKS PUBLISHED BY
OSPREY MILITARY AND AVIATION PLEASE CONTACT:

North America:
Osprey Direct
2427 Bond Street, University Park, IL 60466, USA
Email: **info@ospreydirectusa.com**

All other regions:
Osprey Direct UK
PO Box 140, Wellingborough, Northants, NN8 2FA, UK
Email: **info@ospreydirect.co.uk**

Buy online at **www.ospreypublishing.com**

Dedication

This book is dedicated to the late Hal Giblin.

Acknowledgements

I would like to express my gratitude to my wife Maggie,
to Graham Sumner, and to Roy Wilson for all their help.
Imperial War Museum pictures appear by permission of
the Trustees.

Artist's Note

Readers may care to note that the original paintings from
which the colour plates in this book were prepared are
available for private sale. All reproduction copyright
whatsoever is retained by the Publishers. All enquiries
should be addressed to:

gs.illustrator@binternet.com

The Publishers regret that they can enter into no
correspondence upon this matter.

GERMAN AIR FORCES 1914–18

ORIGINS OF THE ARMY AIR SERVICE

Like all the Great Powers in the years before the outbreak of war, Germany remained uncertain about the direction of its military aviation effort. In the early years of the 20th century balloons were pre-eminent because of their range and large payload, and by 1908 a fleet of Zeppelin dirigible (i.e. steerable) airships was in development. At the same time the Technical Section of the General Staff was also considering the military value of aircraft. The lack of a German aircraft industry slowed progress, but by 1910 the General Staff was coming to the conclusion that the future lay with heavier-than-air craft.

The foundations of the Army Air Service were laid in 1912, when an organizational structure was set down, and the first units were created in the following year. Only Prussia and Bavaria, the two largest states within the Empire, raised aviation units; Saxony formed its own small detachment, but this was attached to a Prussian unit. Five *Flieger Bataillone*, each four companies strong, were created – four on the Royal Prussian establishment, as part of the Communications Branch, and one on the Royal Bavarian establishment. These battalions were not

Oswald Boelcke – the father-figure of German fighter pilots. Boelcke originally served with Telegraphen Bataillon Nr.3 before entering flying school in June 1914. He flew two-seaters with FFA 13 before a transfer to FFA 62 and its single-seater flight. His successes with the Fokker Eindecker brought him fame, decorations, and, in August 1916, command of the newly formed Jasta 2, equipped with fast new Albatros D-Types. He was an inspiring teacher and leader, and after his death at the age of 25 in October 1916 the unit was retitled Jasta Boelcke. Here the strain of combat shows clearly on his face. He wears the field cap of the technical branches, with black band and red piping; and a light grey M1903 officer's greatcoat with mid-blue collar piped red, over a plain-collared tunic – see also photo on page 58. (Imperial War Museum Q58027)

intended for service in the front line as tactical units; rather, each would form a cadre able to supply a flight of aircraft for attachment to every Army and Corps headquarters.

These formations originally transported their aircraft in sections by road, accompanying a column of troops, to be assembled as and when they were needed for a mission. However, when one such craft collapsed in mid-air while on manoeuvres in 1913, killing its crew, this requirement was sensibly abandoned. The remaining craft all needed modification to make them safe, and 1914 began with an acute shortage of aircraft, and thus of newly qualified pilots. By that summer the situation had largely been retrieved, and the flying schools were working at full capacity; nevertheless, measures were still put in place to allow civilian pilots to be sent directly to front line units in times of need.

Table 1: Army Air Service units, July 1914

Prussian	stations	attached to
Luftschiffer Bataillon:		
Nr.1	Berlin (Tegel)	Gardekorps
Nr.2	Berlin, Hannover, Dresden	Gardekorps
Nr.3	Köln, Düsseldorf, Darmstadt	IX Armeekorps
Nr.4	Mannheim, Metz, Lahr, Friedrichshafen	XIV Armeekorps
Nr.5	Graudenz, Königsberg,Scheidemühl	I Armeekorps
Flieger Bataillon:		
Nr.1	Döberitz (HQ & 1.Komp), Jüterbog (2.Komp), Großenhain (3.Komp), (Saxon)	Gardekorps
Nr.2	Posen (HQ & 1.Komp), Graudenz (2.Komp), Königsberg (3.Komp)	V Armeekorps
Nr.3	Köln (HQ & 1.Komp), Hannover (2.Komp), Truppenübungsplatz, Darmstadt (3.Komp)	VIII Armeekorps
Nr.4	Strasburg (HQ & 1.Komp), Metz (2.Komp), Freiburg (3.Komp)	XV Armeekorps
Bavarian		
Luft- u. Kraftfahrer Btl	München	I Bav Armeekorps
Flieger Btl	Oberschleißheim	I Bav Armeekorps

Table 2: Air Service units in the field, 17 August 1914

OHL	seven airships		5.Armee	EFp Nr.5; FLA 4, FFA 25
1.Armee	Etappen Flugpark Nr.1; FLA 1, FFA 12		V Korps	FFA 19
II Korps	FFA 30		XIII Korps	FFA 4
III Korps	FFA 7		XVI Korps	FFA 2
IV Korps	FFA 9			
IX Korps	FFA 11		6.Armee	Bav EFp Nr.6; Bav FLA 1, FFA 5
			XXI Korps	FFA 8
2.Armee	EFp Nr.2; FLA 2, FFA 23		I Bav Korps	Bav FFA 1
Gardekorps	FFA 1		II Bav Korps	Bav FFA 2
VII Korps	FFA 18		III Bav Korps	Bav FFA 3
X Korps	FFA 21			
			7.Armee	EFp 7; FLA 6, FFA 26
3. Armee	EFp Nr.3; FLA 7, FFA 22		XIV Korps	FFA 20
XI Korps	FFA 28		XV Korps	FFA 3
XII Korps	FFA 29			
XIX Korpps	FFA 24		8.Armee	EFp Nr.8; FLA 8, FFA 16;
				airships *Königsberg, Allenstein*
4.Armee	EFp Nr.4; FLA 3, FFA 6			*& Thorn*
VI Korps	FFA 13		I Korps	FFA 14
VIII Korps	FFA 10		XVII Korps	FFA 17
XVIII Korps	FFA 27		XX Korps	FFA 15
			Fortress of Graudenz	Festungsflieger Abteilung

(Note: Cavalry, Reserve and Landwehr formations which did not have attached aviation units are omitted from this Table.)

At the time of mobilization in August 1914, 33 *Feldflieger Abteilungen* (FFA) were created, 30 Prussian and 3 Bavarian. Each of the eight army HQs received one, as did each of the 25 regular army corps HQs (see Table 2); but insufficient pilots and aircraft were available to equip FFAs for the Cavalry Corps or for any of the Reserve corps. Each FFA was equipped with six aircraft, and had a flying strength of seven pilots and six observers, backed up by a ground crew consisting of 116 enlisted men. Each unit maintained a fleet of five touring cars, one tender, six aircraft towing vehicles (for movement between airfields, or for the recovery of crashed machines), as well as workshop lorries, and lorries for transporting stores, munitions, fuel and baggage. Reserves were held in an aircraft park *(Etappen-Flugzeugpark)*, which formed part of each army's lines of communication troops; each park normally held three aircraft, as well as two pilots and one observer. The conversion of fortress units into front line FFAs, and the creation of new FFAs, meant that their original number quickly doubled, and by the beginning of 1915 as many as 60 such units were serving on the various fronts.

Lt Max Immelmann at the scene of one of his victories. Immelmann served in a Saxon railway regiment before transferring to the Air Service; this photo shows clearly the officer's M1910 uniform of the technical branches, with double *Litzen* on red-piped black patches on the black-piped collar, *Litzen* and black piping on the cuffs, and red front piping. Serving with Boelcke in the single-seater flight of FFA 62 at Douai, Immelmann achieved 17 aerial victories, and international fame, before his death in June 1916. (IWM Q58026)

CHRONOLOGY

1914:

August On mobilization, Army Air Service forms eight observation balloon detachments, 15 fortress balloon detachments, 18 crews for the 12 Army airships, and six airship replacement units. Thirty-three field flying detachments (FFA) are mobilized, plus eight fortress flying units and eight aircraft parks, leaving five replacement units at home. A balloon detachment (FLA), an FFA and an aircraft park are allocated to each of the eight armies in the field, and a further FFA to each of the 25 regular army corps.

7–22 August Airships begin bombing raids, against Liège and in support of 6.Armee in Alsace; three are shot down, and a fourth during operations on the Eastern Front. Airships thereafter relegated to night missions only.

23 August Battle of Mons. Aircraft spot British dispositions, but operating over Belgian territory hinders communications and the information fails to reach army commanders in time to affect the course of the battle.

26–30 August Battle of Tannenberg on Eastern Front; reconnaissance aircraft monitor Russian movements, and since flying over German territory, information is passed on more quickly. The Russians are encircled and defeated; Gen Ludendorff later comments, 'No aerial intelligence, no Tannenberg.'

5–10 September Battle of the Marne. Aircraft reveal French advance into gap between two German armies in time for German withdrawal.

October/November Air staff officer *(Stofl)* appointed to each army HQ to co-ordinate FFAs, although their employment remains in the hands of army and corps commanders.

11 November Flying a Rumpler B, Lts Flashar (pilot) and Demuth (observer) bring down a French machine – the first German victory in aerial combat.

1915:

19 January First airship raid against the UK: Navy L3 & L4 drop bombs in Yarmouth area of Norfolk coast. Raids against London follow on 31 May/1 June, and continue intermittently until 19 October 1917.

11 March Maj Hermann Thomsen (later von der Lieth-Thomsen) is appointed to newly created post of Chef des Feldflugwesens (Feldflugchef) to control all aviation units in the field.

21–22 March First airship raids against Paris.

April Bomber unit codenamed Carrier Pigeon Unit, Ostend (Brieftauben Abteilung Ostende, BAO) formed under direct orders of Army High Command (OHL), as bomber reserve, and makes significant contribution to Eastern Front campaign. Second unit formed as BA Metz (BAM).

June First Fokker monoplanes, armed with a forward-firing machine gun, arrive at the front, and a few are attached to existing FFAs.

6/7 June First airship destroyed by RFC; Flt S/Lt R.Warneford of No.1 Sqn RNAS destroys LZ37 over Ghent, Belgium, with air-dropped bombs.

August First dedicated artillery co-operation units – Feldflieger Abteilungen (Artillerie), FFA(A) – are formed, one attached to each corps headquarters.

1 August Flying one of the new Fokker Eindeckers from Douai, Lt Max Immelmann of FFA 62 shoots down a British BE2c – the first official victory with this type. This marks the start of the 'Fokker Scourge', a period of German air superiority that will last until summer 1916.

December Picked crews form two new Kampfgeschwäder der Obersten Heeresleitung (Kagohl), created to replace BAO and BAM and capitalize on their success. Each Kagohl consists of six flights (Staffeln) of six aircraft each. Seven Kagohl will eventually be formed.

1916:

February FFA 'Pascha' formed to serve with Turkish forces in the Middle East.

21 February–10 April During early stage of battle of Verdun, two Kagohl (four by beginning of April), ten FFAs, six FFA(A)s and three temporary units of single-seaters are concentrated in this sector, but are soon outnumbered by French aircraft and lose air superiority.

March Despite relegation of airships to night missions only, losses over the Western Front are such that they force another change of tactics. Henceforth airships concentrate their attacks on English and French ports only. Airships in the East and the Balkans are unaffected, and continue to attack inland targets.

June Initial success of Russian 'Brusilov Offensive' forces diversion of two Kagohl to Eastern Front.

1 July–18 November Battle of the Somme. British air forces, superior both in numbers and in aircraft quality, wrest back air superiority. By forming larger single-seater units, and transferring units north from Verdun, Germans finally regain the initiative.

August New type of unit, the Jagdstaffel (Jasta), is formed to replace temporary single-seater units created during the year. During autumn the Jasta are equipped with new

A group of pilots belonging to FFA 62 and KeK Douai, including Immelmann (front, second right), Boelcke (front, fourth left), and Max Ritter von Mulzer (back, extreme left). (IWM Q63132)

Albatros DI and Halberstadt DII, which help redress the balance in aircraft quality.

October New post of Kommandierender General der Luftstreitkräfte (Kogenluft) is created, with operational responsibility for all Army Air Service units at the front and at home. By 1917 he will also acquire responsibility for observation balloons, anti-aircraft artillery, the Army meteorological service, and for the air defence of Germany. The post is filled in December by GenLt Ernst von Höppner.

At the front, the post of Gruppenführer der Flieger (Grufl) is created, with responsibility for all aviation – including training and supply as well as combat units – within a specific area, usually coterminous with an army corps.

Winter 1916–17 Major reorganization brings all units under army rather than corps HQs. FFAs and FFA(A)s are renamed Flieger Abteilungen (FA) and Flieger Abteilungen (Artillerie) (FAA) respectively. FAs are henceforth responsible for long-range reconnaissance, and FAAs for short-range work and artillery spotting. Henceforth Jastas will be used solely for air fighting. The Kagohl are reduced to three in number and concentrate on strategic bombing, the surplus men and machines forming new Schutzstaffeln (Schusta) with the role of protecting reconnaissance aircraft.

1917:

January AA artillery added to responsibilities of Kogenluft. Appointed to each army is a Kommandeur der Flak (Koflak); reporting to him in each division is a Gruppenkommandeur der Flak (Flakgruko).

April FA 'Pascha' in Mesopotamia is enlarged, then divided into FAs 301–305.

4 April–27 May Battle of Arras. British fail to achieve local air superiority due to confident German handling of new Albatros DIII fighters during 'Bloody April'.

17 April–8 May French 'Nivelle Offensive'. German concentrations draw off French fighters, leaving their reconnaissance machines vulnerable, and many are shot down without fulfilling their mission.

25 May First daylight bomber aircraft attack on UK, by 21 Gotha GIVs of Kagohl 3; most bombs fall on Folkestone, Kent, killing 95 and injuring 260; one Gotha lost. Kagohl 3 makes first daylight raid on London on 13 June, dropping 4 tons-plus, killing 162 and injuring 432. This is followed in September by first night raid. Raids continue intermittently until 19 May 1918.

7 June–10 November Third Battle of Ypres (Passchendaele). The RFC gains air superiority over the battlefield, despite the presence of some 80 German units. British ground advances checked locally by innovative use of Schusta in ground-attack role; bombing raids on airfields nullify French attempts to intervene.

24 June Jagdgeschwader 1 (JG1), a permanent grouping of four Jasta, is formed under command of Rittmeister Manfred von Richthofen.

August 1917–February 1918 The 'Amerikaprogram', prompted by entry of USA into the war in April. Kogenluft instigates ambitious expansion scheme to double the number of fighter units by 1 March 1918. The target is met, but at considerable cost; poorly trained pilots are thrust into action, and planned expansion in number of reconnaissance units is halted.

September New post of Kommandeur der Luftschiffer (Koluft) created at each army HQ, to co-ordinate deployment of balloons.

October–December Italians suffer heavy early losses to Austro-German Caporetto offensive, but their growing resistance forces use of all Air Service units for close ground support, regardless of original role. By the end of 1917 the Germans are just beginning to re-establish air superiority on this front when most units are recalled to the Western Front for the forthcoming Spring Offensive.

A vehicle of Armee Flugpark 5 transporting Albatros DV, number 2016/17, by road in the Argonne. Note the ornate 'T' on the fuselage; this machine was flown by Lt Karl Thom of the Saxon Jasta 21s. Thom was shot down twice – the photo might depict one of those occasions – but survived the war with 27 victories. The black-and-white stripe around the fuselage dates from the period when the Ritter von Schleich commanded this unit. (IWM Q53006)

Table 3: Air units attached to 18.Armee, 21 March 1918

(Note: This is a representative example of the air support provided for ground armies in spring 1918. The 18.Armee was established on the Western Front in December 1917 with troops of Heeresgruppe Woyrsch from the Eastern Front. On 21 March 1918 it was committed to Operation 'Michael', against the British 3rd and 5th Armies, alongside 2. & 17.Armee.)

ARMY TROOPS

Kofl 18:
  FA 23 & 39
  FAA 295
  Bogohl I & IV
  Schlasta 8
  Riesenflugzeug Abteilung 18
  Riesenflugzeug Übungsabt 18
  Armee Wetterwarte 18
  Front Wetterwarte 18
  Armee Flugpark 18
Koflak 18:
Flakgruko 18:
  Flak Batterie 567, 576 (4 guns each)
  Flamga 8, 9, 10, 16, 54, 64, 72, 103,
    171, 172 & 175
  Flak Zug 60, 139
  Kraftwagen Flak Zug 32, 36, 56, 67,
    86, 135 & 136
  Flak Scheinwerfer Zug 240, 403, 405
    & 729
  and 5 independent searchlights
  18 MGs from Flamga 901 & 908
Koluft 23

III KORPS

Grufl 17:
  FAA 234, 245, 247 & 264
  Schlasta 2, 5 & 20
  Jagdgeschwader Nr.1
  Jasta 8, 62 & 68
  Feldluftschiffer Abt 67 (Ballon Zug 33,
    41, 61 & 125)
  Front Wetterwarte 125
  Brieftauben Abt 125

Flakgruko 42:
  Flak Batt 566 (4 guns)
  schw Kraftwagen Flak Batt 127
    (2 guns)
  Flamga 48, 82, 95
  Flak Zug 18, 105, 129
  Kraftwagen Flak Zug 23, 47 & 69
  Flak Scheinwerfer Zug 207 & 698
  8 MGs from Flamga 908

IX KORPS

Grufl 13:
  FAA 237, 271 & 290
  Schlasta 6
  Jagdgruppe Nr.11
  Jasta 17, 22 & 63
  Feldluftschiffer Abt 37 (Ballon Zug 82,
    96 & 118)
  Front Wetterwarte 216
  Brieftauben Abt 216
Flakgruko 7:
  Flak Batt 508 (4 guns)
  schw Kraftwagen Flak Batt 119 & 162
    (2 guns each)
  Flamga 29, 50 & 176
  Flak Zug 19 & 84
  Kraftwagen Flak Zug 80 & 93
  Flak Scheinwerfer Zug 726
  24 MGs from Flamga 912

XVII KORPS

Grufl 8:
  FA 29, FAA 206, 212 & 225
  Schlasta 7, 34 & 37
  Jagdgruppe Nr.5

Jasta 48, 53 & 63
Feldluftschiffer Abt 29 (Ballon Zug 29,
  31, 32, 40, 49 & 127)
Front Wetterwarte 309
Brieftauben Abt 309
Flakgruko 54:
  Flak Batt 517 (4 guns)
  Kraftwagen Flak Batt 121 (2 guns)
  Flamga 12, 22, 86, 104 & 180
  Flak Zug 1 & 78
  Kraftwagen Flak Zug 35 & 102
  Flak Scheinwerfer Zug 180 & 181
  18 MGs from Flamga 912

IV RESERVE KORPS

Grufl 9:
  FAA 216, 226, 254, 287 & 297
  Schlasta 18, 31 & 36
  Jagdgruppe Nr.12
  Jasta 24, 44 & 79
  Feldluftschiffer Abt 11 & 30
    (Ballon Zug 4, 19, 83, 91, 94,
    120 & 126)
  Front Wetterwarte 217 & 218
  Brieftauben Abt 217 & 218
Flakgruko 8:
  Flak Batt 707 (4 guns)
  Kraftwagen Flak Batt 113, 123 & 159
    (2 guns each)
  Flamga 81, 177 & 178
  Flak Zug 30, 121 & 170
  Kraftwagen Flak Zug 6 & 33
  Flak Scheinwerfer Zug 723
  12 MGs from Flamga 901

1918:

2 February JG 2 and JG 3 are formed; like JG 1, each comprises four Jasta.

March Schusta reconnaissance protection flights are renamed Schlachtstaffeln (Schlasta), and reassigned to ground attack and infantry support.

21 March Opening of massive German Spring Offensive. Schlasta play a decisive role locally, but destruction of Allied airfields makes it difficult for forward units to keep up with advances by German infantry. The dislocation of Allied forces achieved during the first few days is soon reversed by their numerical superiority.

May Excellent Fokker DVII fighter begins to arrive in numbers at front line units; but shortages of fuel, transfer of ground crew into the infantry, and aircraft losses all combine to reduce the overall effectiveness of the German effort.

8 August Battle of Amiens. German reconnaissance fails to identify precise location or timing of British offensive, leaving OHL unable to deploy units in the threatened sector in sufficient time or numbers. Jasta pilots inflict heavy losses on bombers attacking the Somme bridges, but cannot prevent them from being destroyed.

12–30 September Battle of St Mihiel. German forces are overwhelmed by the numbers the Allies can bring to bear, and are driven from the skies.

11 November Last German air victories of the war. Lt von Frieden of Jasta 50 brings down a BF2b of 20 Sqn RFC, but precise time goes unrecorded; at 10.50am, Offizier-Stellvertreter Friedrich Altemeier of Jasta 24s shoots down an RE8.

FIELD UNITS

Initially (and to some extent throughout the war), most units consisted of a variety of different aircraft types. In 1915, for example, FFA 23 was equipped with four types: the Albatros DDK, Rumpler 4A13, Gotha Taube and Fokker M8. As a result, a large variety of spare parts had to be kept on charge – a major logistical problem. Britain and France had decided at an early stage to standardize on one type within each squadron. This was never possible in Germany, since production levels within the industry were never able to keep pace, either with the expansion of the service or even with losses in action. Aircraft fresh off the production line were simply sent to wherever the need was most acute. This mixture of aircraft types was of course at its greatest when converting from one type to another: in August 1916 Jasta 1 was operating six different types, while even in September 1918 Jasta 36 had four types.

In the first stages of the war the aircraft of both sides were designed primarily for reconnaissance. In addition to the pilot they included room for an observer, who could make notes on the dispositions of the enemy at a distance far beyond that achieved by the conventional cavalry screen. In the initial engagements both sides made good use of aircraft to spot gaps that could then be exploited by an advance on the ground.

Aircraft were unarmed, and any aerial combats were a matter of opposing crews taking pot-shots at one another with small arms. From April 1915, however, German aircraft found themselves increasingly vulnerable to French scouts carrying a machine gun mounted to fire through the arc of the propeller, by means of a crude arrangement of armoured wedges fitted to the blades. Two technical innovations reversed this trend: the adoption of interrupter gear, an improvement on the French invention which genuinely synchronized the fire of the new LMG08 machine gun with propeller revolutions; and the introduction of a lighter hand-traversed LMG14 for the observers in reconnaissance machines.

Early in the war, a Taube monoplane leaves its tented hangar and prepares to take off from an airfield somewhere in France. The presence of the ambulance vehicle may or may not have been reassuring to the pilot and observer.

The new interrupter gear was mounted on the highly manoeuvrable Fokker monoplane (Eindecker), and one or two of the newly equipped machines were attached to each FFA to provide escorts for reconnaissance aircraft. But the progressive arming of reconnaissance machines also meant that they could now defend themselves, and Eindecker pilots were increasingly sent up on interception missions.

With the change from mobile to static ground warfare, the aircraft of the FFAs were also called upon increasingly to undertake other roles – bombing, and spotting for artillery fire, as well as

An observer with his LMG14 machine gun, the position of its traversing ring forcing him to crouch down inside the cockpit. Both observer and pilot are wearing the regulation padded helmets. Note also the rack of signal pistol flares on the fuselage side. (IWM Q23896)

short and long range reconnaissance. Such a mix of roles, combined with the variety of aircraft on strength, reduced effectiveness. There were also inefficiencies in the way that reconnaissance information was handled at Army HQ level, and it became clear that the Air Service was not operating to its full potential.

Reconnaissance units

The answer lay in specialization. The first step in that direction came in August 1915 with the creation of a new type of unit, the Feldflieger Abteilung (Artillerie) – FFA(A) – for the specific purpose of working with the artillery. Fifteen such units (12 Prussian, three Bavarian) were formed, each consisting of four to six aircraft, and were allocated to corps HQs or to local artillery commanders. Next, from February 1916 onwards, single-seat fighter aircraft were withdrawn to form their own units.

Meanwhile, the two-seaters of the remaining FFAs continued with their tactical bombing and reconnaissance work. Both types of unit continued to grow in number: by the beginning of 1916, 74 Prussian FFAs and 40 FFA(A)s were in service, with Bavaria contributing a further nine and three respectively. The aircraft on strength in 1914 were gradually replaced by various models of the C-Type – a two-seater, single-engined aircraft, armed with one fixed machine gun firing forward, and a second, on a pivot attached to a rotatable ring, which covered the sides and rear in the hands of the observer in the rear cockpit.

In January 1917 the units were all renamed – as Flieger Abteilung (FA) and Flieger Abteilung (Artillerie) (FAA) respectively – and renumbered. In the spring of the same year a second

An observer leans over the side of his Euler-built Albatros two-seater to take a photograph.

A camouflage-painted AEG CIV, number 2054/17, with reconnaissance camera. Despite the date note that the crew still wear the pre-war padded helmet; and that two men are crammed into the rear cockpit. The AEG C-Types were stubby, ungainly looking machines, but they did sterling work with the FAs and FAAs from their introduction in 1916 until virtually the end of the war. (IWM Q60316)

reorganization took place that redistributed the FAs. One FA was now attached to each army HQ in an operational reconnaissance role. Another, tasked with tactical reconnaissance and long range artillery spotting, was attached to each corps HQ, while an FAA served with each division HQ. Most FAAs also included aircraft specifically tasked to co-operate with ground forces (Infanterieflieger); it was one of their duties to monitor the progress of an attack, noting enemy positions, and reporting back to corps or army headquarters. An elaborate scheme of signals permitted two-way communication between aircraft and front line troops. The FAAs were also able to undertake a limited amount of resupply by air. The location of any bottlenecks would be passed on, to become the responsibility of the Schusta.

The instructions to Infanterieflieger laid emphasis on regular photographic sorties, at least once a week, and on maintaining regular contact with the infantry – again, at least once a week in quiet periods. Flying at heights as low as 150ft, the crews were to update situation maps in the air, and transfer the information on to 1:10,000 maps on their return. Information was to be transmitted direct to division, bypassing regimental headquarters.

By this time every FAA aircraft was equipped with a Telefunken telegraph transmitting set, maintaining communications with the divisional artillery commander, who was based back at the FAA's home airfield. According to British intelligence the high water mark of aircraft/artillery work came in January–February 1917, when German artillery made a great number of long and uninterrupted shoots, controlled by aircraft. Experience laid emphasis on the need for close co-operation between aircraft and the divisional artillery commander, and special liaison officers were appointed to co-ordinate communications. Night ranging was introduced in the autumn of 1917, but this could only be used against large targets, particularly those with strong daytime anti-aircraft defences, such as crossroads, camps or railway stations.

The introduction of the Reihenbildner camera in 1916 was a major step forward in photographic reconnaissance. Older models required the observer to expose a succession of single glass plate negatives manually; this new type of camera was automatic, driven by a small

windmill generator that turned in the airflow, exposing negatives onto a roll of film. With later models containing sufficient film to photograph approximately 300 square miles of terrain, the Reihenbildner made it possible to record a mosaic of the Allied lines instead of individual positions. Operating at approximately 18,000ft, the Rumpler CIVs and CVIIs that carried these cameras were usually too high to attract interference from Allied fighters. Initially, one of these specially equipped aircraft was allocated to each FA as they came off the production line; but from September 1917 they were organized into their own units (there were eventually 15 altogether), denoted by the suffix 'Lb' ('mit Lichtbildgerät') and normally attached to army HQs.

By 1918 at least one FA Lb was attached to OHL, and another to each army HQ. Each army HQ also included one FA for long distance reconnaissance, to locate the enemy reserves (known colloquially as 'AOK flights'),

A line-up of Albatros DVs at Roucourt airfield, near St Quentin, in April 1917. These appear to be aircraft from several different units, including Jasta 3, 4, 11 and 33. The aircraft second from the front was flown by Manfred von Richthofen of Jasta 11. (IWM Q50328)

and another for heavy artillery ranging. Each corps HQ had an FA for the reconnaissance of the rear of the enemy immediately opposite, and for some artillery or infantry co-operation work; and each division HQ controlled an FA for tactical reconnaissance and infantry co-operation.

The importance of aerial photography was quickly recognized. Each army staff had a photographic interpretation officer responsible for evaluating the information received, passing it on to local commanders

and updating the cartographic unit. As the amount of work grew, however, one man was no longer sufficient and in 1917 the post was expanded into a whole section, the Stabsbild Abteilung (Stabia). Centralizing the interpretation work in this way had its advantages, but units at the front were still not receiving the information quickly enough. Temporary group photographic sections allowed the new Grufls to evaluate the reports covering their territory; by April 1918 each Grufl had at his disposal a permanent photographic section, speedily distributing local information for regimental commanders, before sending it up the line to the Stabia for further evaluation and inclusion in the army's maps. Hans Schröder, serving as a Grufl with Gruppe Wytschaete in 1917, boasted that the photos he requested were delivered to him just one hour after the reconnaissance aircraft took off.

Close support units

For the start of the Verdun offensive in February 1916 the Germans assembled ten FFAs, six FFA(A)s, two specially strengthened Kagohl and three fighter units, as well as four airships and 21 observation balloons. The number of aircraft they put into the sky allowed them to achieve air superiority for a short time, before the French countered with even more machines, including increasing numbers of the agile new Nieuport 11. This forced the Germans to divert two-seater units from their proper functions of reconnaissance and tactical bombing, to throw them instead into the air superiority battle, or use them as escorts for reconnaissance missions, or in ground attacks in support of the infantry – tasks for which they were not equipped. As a result the units suffered high losses in both men and machines and were unable to fulfil their intended role of harassing the enemy's rear.

The same pattern repeated itself on the Somme later that year. On 1 July the Germans were able to muster only five FFAs, four FFA(A)s, two fighter detachments and one Kagohl. These were quickly overwhelmed by the opposing Allied forces, which were superior both in quality and quantity. Reinforcements were drawn in over the next few months until, by October 1916, there were 26 FFAs, 20 FFA(A)s, 33 bomber Staffeln and four fighter units operating over that sector of the front.

The initial German response was to create a new type of unit that could be used in a dual role, providing escorts for reconnaissance machines as well as undertaking local ground attack duties, leaving the other units free to concentrate on their proper roles. The new units were named Schutzstaffeln (Schusta) – 'protection flights' – and 38 were created in the winter of 1916–17 by disbanding specialist bomber flights. But finding aircraft capable of performing effectively in both roles was a problem. The Schusta were at first equipped with the same C-Types as the FFAs, but these were insufficiently robust for ground attack work. G-Type aircraft – twin-engined and armed with a number of machine guns – were better able to perform ground attack duties and could defend themselves if attacked, but they were too heavy and unwieldy to perform well as escort machines, and were soon transferred to bombing missions.

The choice eventually fell on single-engined aircraft like the Halberstadt CLII and IV or the Hannover CLII and III: over the winter of 1917–18 each Schusta was equipped with six such aircraft, with a total strength of 67 men. Each unit was attached to a division HQ, principally for escort work, but some aircraft within each unit were also made available on a stand-by basis for infantry or artillery co-operation duties. After some success in ground support work in 1917 – particularly during the battle of Arras in April under Hptm Zorer of Schusta 7 – the escort role was finally abandoned, leaving the Schusta free at last to concentrate on ground attack.

The Halberstadts and Hannovers were eventually supplemented by the armoured Junkers J1, built especially for the ground attack role and introduced in 1918. Problems of communication had to be overcome before these aircraft could be used to their full potential. Infantry battalions included a lamp signalling section, but this was not always effective on a smoke-shrouded battlefield. Equally, flares and Bengal lights could sometimes be difficult to see in bright sunlight. The strips of cloth given to ground troops to mark their positions and construct simple signals quickly became dirty and unreadable; even when clean they also advertised the position to Allied flyers. The aircraft had to drop their messages to the front line troops, at the same time using their telegraph to communicate with division HQ. Once a bottleneck in the advance had been reported to army or corps headquarters, the Grufl could allocate units to attack the enemy position. Using wireless telegraphy speeded up the whole process, and aircraft could be allocated a new objective while they were still in the air, rather than waiting for them to return to their home airfield.

For the March 1918 offensive the 38 Schusta were renamed Schlachtstaffel (Schlasta) – 'attack flights'. This was more in keeping with their actual battlefield role, which was described in some detail in the *Manual of Positional Warfare*. The *Manual* recommended that Army HQs should retain some Schlasta to harass traffic in the enemy's rear areas; others should be controlled by corps HQs to use during the latter stages of the battle, when they would be required to break up pockets of resistance or counter-attacks; but most should be employed by division HQs on their immediate front, 'to ensure their being engaged at the right moment'. It also argued that the lower the Schlasta aircraft flew, the greater not only was the moral effect on the enemy, but also the material effect on his front line, and for this reason it advocated

descents to between 150 and 90 feet. For the engagement of larger targets (e.g. reserves and batteries) a height of 1,200–1,500ft was regarded as more favourable. The *Manual* further recommended that the Schlasta should not be spread along the whole length of the front, but concentrated at decisive points. For large-scale operations, units should attack in waves rather than all at once. In his memoirs, Gen Ludendorff described the Schlasta in action:

> These [aircraft] would dive from high in the sky and fly low over the ground. They would attack with machine guns and light bombs the enemy infantry, artillery and, as occurred more and more, the enemy reserves also, columns and trains as well as columns of march coming from far away. Originally intended as an ancillary infantry weapon, at the end these Schlasta were also given great tactical tasks... Like the other combat weapons, they too were weapons of destruction in the great land battle. This was their purpose – the battle in the air remained only a means to that end.

Although they met with some success in the first few days of the offensive, this was only temporary; when the Allies countered by using low-level aircraft of their own, the work of the Schlasta was severely disrupted. Nevertheless, their overall contribution, both in material terms and in the heightened morale of the ground troops they supported, was sufficient to prompt the diversion of newly qualified fighter pilots to the Schlasta in the summer of 1918. An additional 22 Schlasta were to be formed in this way, making a total of ten Geschwäder of six Staffeln each. In the event, only two of the proposed Staffeln were formed; nevertheless, the remaining units continued to disrupt Allied concentrations until the end of the war.

The ground support tactics first developed during the war were perfected during 1919 by the former Navy fighter pilot Gotthard Sachsenburg, with the flying units of the Freikorps in the Baltic states.

A photo allegedly taken just before Manfred von Richthofen's last flight on 21 April 1918; Richthofen is the fourth pilot from the right. Dark-coloured flying suits appear to be the favoured clothing in this group of JG 1 pilots; and note the harness of the Heinicke parachute worn by several of them. The squadron buildings are a haphazard mixture of wooden huts, corrugated 'elephant' iron and tents. (IWM Q63136)

Among the troops on the ground who benefited from that air support was a certain Hptm Heinz Guderian.

FIGHTER UNITS

The new interrupter gear and lightweight air-cooled LMG08 machine gun found their ideal vehicle in the Fokker Eindecker monoplane, which was far more manoeuvrable than anything else in the skies in 1915. Flying a handful of these machines, officers such as Immelmann, Boelcke and Kastner of FFA 62 became the world's first true fighter pilots.

The development of a specialist fighter aircraft called for new tactics. Instead of acting as the escort and protector of two-seaters, the Fokkers now set off on missions with the sole aim of destroying enemy machines. Sometimes alone, more often with a wingman, the Fokker pilots would stalk their opponents, using cloud cover whenever possible, and then close in swiftly to deliver the telling blow: 'I fly close to my man, aim well, and then of course he falls down', Oswald Boelcke told the young Richthofen.

To counter these 'hunting' missions, the Allies attached one or two machines as an escort to their reconnaissance aircraft. From the spring of 1916 this led in turn to the formation of dedicated German flights to oppose them: these were the Kampfeinsitzer-Kommandos (KeK) – 'fighting single-seater commands' – each composed of up to four single-seaters, withdrawn from their parent FFAs and based at a single airfield. The new KeK drove the French from the skies over Verdun at a vital moment, and gave the British a hard time before they could introduce new fighters of their own.

Table 4: Deployment of Jagdstaffeln, 1 December 1916

Higher formation & airfield	Jasta number	Formed from	Higher formation & airfield	Jasta number	Formed from
1.Armee (north of Rheims)			*6.Armee (Picardy)*		
Gonnelieu	5	KeK Staffel A	Brayelles-Douai	11	6.Armee
Lagnicourt	2	Flieger Ersatz Abteilung 7	Riencourt	12	Fokkerstaffel West
Neuflize-Le Chatelet	21	Armee Flugpark 3	*7.Armee (Eastern Champagne)*		
Proville	1	KeK Nord & FAs of 1.Armee	Leffincourt	9	Armeestaffel des AOK 3
Riencourt	22	FFA 11 & 29, FAA 22			
2.Armee (Somme)			*Armee Abteilung A (Alsace)*		
Neuflize-Le Chatelet	20	Armee Flugpark 2	Metz-Frescaty	17	Armee Flugpark 5
Fontaine-Uterte	3	Flieger Ersatz Abteilung 5	Ronssoy	19	Armee Flugpark 1
Roupy	4	KeK Vaux	Mörchingen	24	Armee Abteilung A
Ugny l'Equipée	6	Fokkerstaffel Sivry			
3.Armee (Champagne)	(none)		*Armee Abteilung B (Lorraine)*		
			Habsheim	15	KeK Habsheim
4.Armee (Flanders)			Ensisheim	16	KeK Ensisheim, FA 9b
Neuvilly-Le Cateau	8	FEA 10, FA 6,33 & 40, FAA 213			
			Armee Abteilung Stranz (Alsace)		
Halluin	18	FEA 12	Mars-la-Tour	13	Armee Abteilung C
5.Armee (Verdun)			(forming at Pusieux)	23	Armee Abteilung Stranz
Procher	7	Fokkerstaffel Martincourt			
Jametz-Stenay	10	KeK 3	*Macedonia*		
Marchais	14	Falkenhausen Fokkerkampfstaffel	Prilip	25	

The success of the KeK so impressed Kogenluft that in August 1916 they became permanent formations, allocated extra aircraft and renamed Jagdstaffeln (Jasta) – 'hunting flights'. The Jasta remained the basic fighter unit for the remainder of the war. The superiority of the new Albatros over enemy machines forced the Allies to use even larger escorts, and the Germans responded by employing larger formations still. In June 1917, four Jasta (4, 6, 10 & 11) were formed into Jagdgeschwader Nr.1 under Manfred von Richthofen's command. This – like the bomber units BAO and BAM before it – was an elite reserve unit, thrown into battle wherever the fighting was at its most fierce.

The Jasta was larger than the other aviation units, with 14 aircraft, but like the various Abteilungen it was commanded by a first lieutenant or captain. Each aircraft had its own fitter and two riggers, while another 14 mechanics, electricians, joiners, leather workers and cable splicers were employed in general aircraft maintenance. Altogether there were 127 men and 12 vehicles on the strength of each Jasta.

Experience gained in the battles of 1917 demonstrated the value of air superiority as an integral part of the army's effort, whether defensive or offensive, and four more Jagdgeschwäder (three Army, one Navy) were formed in 1918. The principle was not, however, taken to its full conclusion, and not

Table 5: Highest scoring Jagdstaffeln

Scores are for officially confirmed victories over all enemy craft, including balloons. Some victories may have gone unrecorded in the last days of the war; units affected by this included Jasta 28. All records for Jasta 48, 82, 84w, 85, 86, 87, 88, 89 & 90 appear to have been lost.

The date of formation is that of the order that created each Jasta; under normal circumstances, a unit would take the field about two weeks later. The figures for pilots lost include those killed in accidents and those posted as missing.

Jasta	Victories	Formation date	Killed + captured
11	350	28 Sept 1916	19 + 2 POW
2	336	10 Aug 1916	33 + 2 POW
5	253	10 Aug 1916	22 + 2 POW
6	201	25 Aug 1916	12 + 3 POW
4	192	25 Aug 1916	11 + 2 POW
26	180	14 Dec 1916	5 + 1 POW
12	156	8 Oct 1916	17 + 1 POW
36	156	11 Jan 1917	14 + 2 POW
10	151	28 Sept 1916	21 + 4 POW
15	150	28 Sept 1916	9 + 2 POW
21s	141	25 Oct 1916	8 + 1 POW
27	134	5 Feb 1917	14 + 1 POW
7	126	23 Aug 1916	13
45	113	11 Dec 1917	4
18	112	30 Oct 1916	8 + 1 POW
13	109	28 Sept 1916	13 + 2 POW
1	107	22 Aug 1916	13 + 1 POW
9	107	28 Sept 1916	18
MFJ 1	104	1 Feb 1917	15
17	101	23 Oct 1916	12
28w	100	14 Dec 1916	9 + 1 POW

The most successful Bavarian Jasta was 34b (formed 20 Feb 1917), with 89 victories at a cost of 12 killed + 5 captured. The lowest-scoring Jasta of all was 75 (formed 14 Feb 1918), with four victories at a cost of two men killed.

(Source: Franks et al, *Above the Lines*)

The 'Red Baron's' younger brother Lothar von Richthofen in the cockpit of a Fokker DrI triplane. He survived the war, scoring 40 victories, only to be killed while flying a commercial aircraft in 1922. Here he seems to wear a double-breasted leather jacket of the old transport driver type with a large fleece collar. (IWM Q63155)

every Jasta became part of such a large formation. Concerned that there were too few leaders of the quality of Richthofen, with the ability to command effectively a unit of this size, Kogenluft erred on the side of caution. Instead a number of Jagdgruppen were formed during the final year of the war, bringing various Jasta together as the tactical situation required but not on the permanent basis enjoyed by the Jagdgeschwäder.

Tactics

The basic tactical unit in the air was the Kette of two aircraft – a leader and his wingman. Further machines flew echeloned back, above and below. Although aircraft naturally lost formation during a dogfight, commanders nevertheless placed great emphasis on the underlying need for discipline. Leutnant von Wedel, commanding Jasta 7, told his men that during combat, 'the leading principle was to extricate a comrade in a critical situation... After each fight, machines must rally and resume formation... Strict discipline increases mutual confidence... Attack only on the leader's signal. Keep the leader in sight... Never glide or dive in a straight line... If you lose the formation, then return to the aerodrome.'

Table 6: The leading fighter aces

(Note: KIA = killed in action; POW = captured)

Army Air Service	Jasta & JGr/JG	Victories
Rtm Manfred von Richthofen (KIA 21.4.18)	2, 11 & JG1	80
Oblt Ernst Udet	15, 37, 11, 4	62
Oblt Erich Löwenhardt (KIA 10.8.18)	10	54
Lt Josef Jacobs	12, 22s, 7	48
Lt Werner Voss (KIA 23.9.17)	2, 5, 29, 14, 10	48
Lt Fritz Rumey (KIA 27.9.18)	2, 5	45
Hptm Rudolph Berthold	KeK V, Jasta 4, 18 & JG2	14, 44
Hptm Bruno Lörzer	17, 26 & JG3	44
Lt Paul Bäumer	5, 2	43
Hptm Oswald Boelcke (KIA 28.10.16)	FA 62, Jasta 2	40
Lt Franz Büchner	9, 13	40
Oblt Lothar von Richthofen	11	40
Lt Heinrich Gontermann (KIA 30.10.17)	5, 15	39
Oblt Carl Menckhoff (POW 25.7.18)	3, 72s	39
Lt Julius Buckler	17	36
Lt Max von Müller (KIA 9.1.18)	2, 28w	36
Lt Karl Bolle	28w, 2	35
Lt Gustav Dörr	45	35
Lt Otto Könnecke	25, 5	35
Hptm Eduard von Schleich	21, 32b & JGr 8	35
Lt Emil Thuy	21s, 28 & JGr 7	35
Lt Joseph Veltjens	14, 18, 15	35
Marine Air Service		
ObltzS Theodor Osterkamp	MFJ 1, 2	32
ObltzS Gotthard Sachsenberg	MFJ 1	31

(Source: Franks et al, *Above the Lines*)

Lt Ernst Udet of Jasta 4 – with 62 confirmed victories, the highest-scoring German ace to survive the war – poses with his Fokker DVII, the outstanding fighter type of 1918. His personal marking was a large white 'LO!', referring to his fiancée Eleanore Zink. Udet joined the Württemburg Army before transferring to the Air Service; after the war he became famous as a stunt pilot, explorer and international aviation playboy. Over-promoted by Göring in the late 1930s, Gen Udet found his false position intolerable, and shot himself on 17 November 1941. (IWM Q63153)

When a number of Jasta were operating together, each unit flew at a different altitude, one above the other, and (ideally) partly concealed by cloud or the glare of the sun. When the enemy engaged the lowest formation, then the upper formations – usually the Jagdgeschwäder, operating above 12,000 feet – would join in to tilt the balance of numbers. The unit leader was usually the first to attack, with his men behind him arranged in order of experience. This was the way some pilots accumulated large numbers of victories, while others did not. It was more important to be a good marksman than a good pilot, as even Richthofen was forced to admit.

Jasta pilots did not engage in regular offensive patrols of the kind familiar to the British; in the strategic sense theirs was a defensive war. *The Principles of Command in the Defensive Battle*, a manual published by OHL in March 1917, argued that the best means of securing and retaining command of the air was to allot permanently defined areas to the Jasta or groups of single-seaters, whose duty was to attack and destroy or chase away hostile aeroplanes or balloons. Accordingly, the pilots normally kept themselves at readiness at the airfield. Some scanned the air over the front with binoculars to try to spot enemy aircraft; a more reliable method was to wait for information from a chain of observation posts stationed in the front line. Their reports were telephoned to the army Kofl, who would then scramble aircraft to meet any potential threat.

Since the Germans fought over their own lines they had the advantage of fuel and weather. Any aircraft running short of fuel could use the prevailing westerly wind to try to regain the German lines, or even his own airfield, whereas Allied pilots in the same position frequently had to fly into a headwind. Whenever a German pilot survived the downing of his machine, he could return to his unit, and with luck his aircraft could be salvaged; a British or French pilot in the same situation not only lost his aircraft but was also much more likely to be taken prisoner. Instructions issued to 7th Army in March 1917 emphasized that 'the enemy must be engaged over the German lines, he must be attacked with the greatest energy and pursued until the zone of fire of the enemy anti-aircraft batteries is reached.'

Parachutes

German aircrew had another advantage over their Allied counterparts: the availability of parachutes. These were supplied to aircrew during the last seven months of the war, first to the Jasta in late March 1918, and later to two-seater units as well. The Heinicke parachute was invented by one Uffz Heinicke of Feldluftschiffer Abteilung 23, who wanted to improve upon the Paulus parachute, then used only by the crews of observation balloons (see 'Observation Balloons'

Lt Hans Joachim Wolff – like his CO Manfred von Richthofen, a transfer from the lancers – with his pet wolfhound; note the Iron Cross First Class and pilot's badge pinned to the left breast of his *Ulanka* tunic. Known as 'Little Wolf' to distinguish him from his squadron mate Kurt Wolff, he served with Jasta 11, and was killed on 16 May 1918 at the age of 22, after scoring 10 victories in two months while flying the Fokker triplane. (IWM Q63154)

A group of pilots in Macedonia, mostly from Jasta 25, all wearing variations on the fur- or fleece-lined three-quarter length cloth flying coat. At right is Gerhard Fieseler, who later became an aircraft designer; his most famous product was the Fi 156 Storch reconnaissance aircraft of World War II. (IWM Q63139)

below). The new pattern differed from its predecessor by its use of a 'seat cushion' pack hooked to the harness, and a static line from the pack which was attached either to the interior of the cockpit or to the ring of an observer's machine gun mount. The harness consisted of a strong waist belt with attachment D-rings at the hips, and straps passing both over the shoulders and around the upper thighs.

The first man to use the new model was Vfw Weimar of Jasta 56, who successfully baled out of his burning Albatros DVa on 1 April 1918. However, of the 70 or so men who followed, about a third were killed. A design fault may have been to blame: the canopy was too small, and the material of the harness was insufficiently strong, causing it to fail if the parachute opened at speeds greater than 80mph – reached by a pilot only seconds after leaving his plane. Many men made their own modifications to the harness, to try to reduce the impact on the body when the parachute opened and to improve the strength of the harness, particularly the leg straps. Even so, the static line could easily snag the tail assembly, dragging the airman down, while a burning aircraft could also set the canopy on fire.

Aces and decorations

In the early stages of the war, and even when Boelcke and Immelmann were beginning to attract attention flying Eindekkers in summer 1915, aerial combat was a rarity and it was something of a feat to bring down an enemy machine. In November 1915, when both Boelcke and Immelmann had scored six victories each, they were awarded the Knight's Cross with Swords of the Royal Hohenzollern House Order. This was one of Germany's highest awards, previously granted to only three other servicemen (two soldiers and one sailor). Boelcke and Immelmann became famous not only within Air Service circles but also to a wider public. In effect, this was the start of the rise of the 'air ace'. In an era of massed battles by vast armies, it was easier for the public at home to identify with the name of a particular airman as a hero, especially when the very idea of flying was still so novel. It was also easier for Army public relations to promote such an individual. Towards the end of 1915, industrialists in Germany sponsored the manufacture of silver Ehrenbecher ('honour goblets'), and presented them to every pilot and observer officially credited with a kill. (On a more personal level, Max Immelmann – the 'Eagle of Lille' – was receiving 40 letters a day from admirers.) Naval flyers received something similar; however, their award, in the form of a statuette, could be presented for any meritorious act – for example, LtzS Eisenlohr was honoured for the bombing and sinking of the Russian destroyer *Stroiny* in the Gulf of Riga on 22 August 1917.

In January 1916 both Boelcke and Immelmann scored their eighth victories. So incredible did this feat seem to contemporaries that a further honour was deemed necessary, and both were presented with the Pour le Mérite, the famous 'Blue Max', Germany's highest award. They were invited to dine with the King of Bavaria, and received telegrams of congratulation from many of Germany's ruling princes. But both continued to shoot down enemy aircraft and add to their number of kills: Immelmann reached 15 before he was shot down himself on 18 June 1916, while Hptm Boelcke's total would eventually reach 40 before he died in a mid-air collission on 28 October that year. Other pilots, too, began to achieve eight victories: Lt Kurt Wintgens (30 June 1916), Lt Max von Mulzer (8 July), Lt Otto Parschau (9 July), Lt Walter Höhndorf (15th July) and Lt Wilhelm Frankel (9 August). As the precedent of awarding the Pour le Mérite for eight victories had been created, these men duly received the same decoration.

The nature of the 'Blue Max' meant that for the recipients there was no other prize that the authorities could bestow to recognize the achievement of those who went on to reach higher scores. Further, it was available only to commissioned officers, so successful NCO pilots – such

A group photo of pilots from Jasta 26, including Oblt Hermann Göring (centre, with stick) and his close friend Bruno Lörzer (standing, fourth left). Göring was credited with 22 victories, although modern research casts doubt on the validity of some of his claims. Lörzer was another leading World War I ace who would prove inadequate in a senior command in World War II – as, notoriously, would Göring himself. Lörzer was given command of the bombers of II Fliegerkorps on the Channel Coast in 1940. (IWM Q69207)

as Vfw Friedrich Altemeier of Jasta 24s (21 victories), or Vfw Oskar Hennrich of Jasta 46 (20 victories) – were ineligible, even though they had far surpassed the requisite number of aircraft destroyed. By the end of the war the achievements of 1915 had become almost commonplace; so many pilots had reached the qualifying mark of eight victories that it was raised to 16 in January 1917, and then – after Richthofen had reached this target in that very month – to 20. Even the Ehrenbecher were no longer made from silver, but from steel.

By making aerial victories virtually the sole qualification for the award of the Pour le Mérite, the authorities also perhaps over-favoured fighter pilots. By the end of the war a total of 75 awards had been made to the Army Air Service: 59 to fighter pilots, but only eight to men from two-seater units (the other awards went to Kogenluft, his chief of staff, five Bogohl commanders and one balloon observer). Hans Schröder, looking back on his time with FFA 6 on the Eastern Front, did not approve: 'Decorations may have shown themselves a necessary institution... but they are a serious danger to good comradeship... they cannot help but turn the best of comrades into rivals... In the course of the war this bestowal of orders reached such a point of absurdity that no person more or less in possession of his five wits set the slightest store by them.' There were cases of very successful pilots proving unsuited to command a Jasta when subsequently appointed to that responsibility.

Victory claims were rigorously checked and annotated. When the pilot returned to his airfield he would compile a combat report that was sent to his commanding officer. From here, it went on up the chain of command as far as Kogenluft, and for the claim to be allowed it had to be approved at each level. If successful, the pilot was issued with a document detailing the combat, and giving the victory number for himself and for his unit. When the wreckage fell on the German side of the lines the victor was awarded a *diesseit* ('this side') victory. If it fell on enemy territory, but was seen to crash – for example, by a forward observer from the artillery or from a balloon – then it was referred to as a *jenseit* ('their side') victory. Both types counted towards the total of victories (in two-seater units, both pilot and observer added one to their tally). If, however, the enemy plane had been seen to land and could be recovered by the enemy, then the victory was classified as *zur Landung gezwungen*: it counted towards the flyer's total score, but was not given a victory number. Disputed victories were settled at Kofl level; those that could not be resolved were given to the unit, but not to any individual. Victories were not recorded as shared between different pilots.

STRATEGIC BOMBING

Airships

The Army had been operating balloons since 1884. Its first preference was for a semi-rigid type that could accompany troops on the march, and could be assembled and inflated when needed. However, Count Zeppelin's successful demonstration of the endurance and airworthiness of his rigid-framed design led to a change of policy. A fleet of 15 airships of this model was commissioned in 1908, and provision made for the existing two-company-strong Luftschiffer Bataillon to be increased to

Navy Zeppelin L9 at its shed. Commanded by Kapitänleutnant Mathy, this craft took part in the raids on Tyneside on 14 April 1915 and on Hull on 6 June. Just visible on the top profile of the envelope, above the airship number, is the exposed machine gun post. (IWM Q58451)

Navy Zeppelins L11, L12 and L13 in flight. L12 crashed and burned at Ostend on 10 August 1915, little more than six weeks after being commissioned and after only one operational sortie. The other two, after a total of 35 sorties between them, were dismantled in 1917. (IWM Q58452)

three battalions. The newly raised battalions included small contingents from Saxony and Württemberg, and Bavaria also raised its own battalion.

Like the Flieger Bataillonen, these battalions served only as cadres, and on mobilization they formed 18 separate units, each with one airship. Each unit consisted of 3 officers and 146 men, 1 motor car, 2 lorries and 5 horses. The crew of each airship consisted of a commander, a flight engineer, a navigator, a wireless operator, an armaments officer, two helmsmen and between four and eight mechanics, depending on the number of engines on the craft.

The airships were intended primarily for use in operational reconnaissance for OHL. In addition to its normal crew, each airship was to have on board a staff officer who would take command of the craft after departure. Under optimum weather conditions, a range of around 300 miles was expected at a cruising speed of 40 miles per hour. Operations were planned to take place in daylight, although some provision had also been made for night-time bombing.

However, the German Navy took a different view. It had quickly seen the potential of the airship as a strategic bomber and, soon after the outbreak of war, began pressing the Kaiser for permission to launch air raids over England. This was granted on 7 January 1915, with the proviso that attacks should be restricted to military targets. The first raid took place on the night of 19/20 January, when two out of three airships reached the Norfolk coast and dropped bombs on the ports of Great Yarmouth and King's Lynn.

Naval airship crews consisted of a Kapitän-Leutnant in command, accompanied by an Oberleutnant or Leutnant zur See as second-in-command (Wachoffizier). The navigator and engineer were warrant officers, while six

ratings were variously responsible for the elevators (two), the steering (two), the wireless (one) and fabric repair (one). The crew also included engineer ratings, usually two per engine, and sometimes an extra rating responsible for the fuel supply. Each airship had its own maintenance party (Schiffspflegegruppe) of 24 men divided into two watches. Neither Army nor Navy airships carried parachutes; lack of space meant that the packs had to be slung outside the gondolas, and – since all airships were filled with highly flammable hydrogen – the chances of making a safe descent from a burning airship were considered by the crews to be so remote that parachutes were abandoned, and the weight saved was used to increase the bomb load.

Experience in action quickly revealed endemic problems. Airships were too slow and, laden with bombs, flew too low to escape Allied fire. An attempt by three Army airships to bomb Paris in March 1915 met with only limited success – SL2 turned back before reaching the main target, bombing nothing more than targets of opportunity in Champagne; ZX was shot down by ground fire over St Quentin on the return leg, and only LZ35 reached its base again. Nor could airships offer much in the way of tactical support. An attempt to disrupt French replacements for the Verdun front by bombing Nancy on 22 February 1916 was a failure; only one craft reached the target, two were forced to turn back by bad weather (one of them being wrecked in a crash landing), and one was shot down.

The Army became disenchanted with the airship, and in 1917 turned over all its remaining machines to the Navy. Between 1915 and 1918, flying over the undefended North Sea, airships made 53 attacks on the United Kingdom, dropping a total of 5,751 bombs.

In total 73 dirigible airships (59 Zeppelins, eight Schütte-Lanz and six other types) saw service with the German forces. Seventeen were lost during raids, while six more were destroyed on 5 January 1918 in a fire at the headquarters of the Naval Airship Division at Ahlorn in north-west Germany. As a weapon of war they were ineffective. They demanded careful handling by their crews, making replacement personnel hard to find and difficult to train to the level required. Nor were the craft wholly reliable. Allied defences obliged the Germans to fly at high altitudes, resulting in many engine failures. At the same time, splits in the fabric were frequent, causing a loss of hydrogen – or worse, a potentially explosive mixture of hydrogen and air. Navigation, too, was always difficult. Many Navy captains had seen service in the merchant marine, and were used to navigating by the stars, but in other than perfect weather conditions they often had to fall back on dead reckoning. Many craft lost their way, and had either to turn back or jettison their bombs. Finally, bomb sights were not accurate enough to ensure that only military targets were hit. Airship raids still had some effect, causing panic amongst the civilian population and undermining morale, but they did not materially affect the outcome of the war. Indeed, it could be argued that British public outrage over the deliberate bombing of cities, and consequent vengefulness, outweighed any German gains.

Aircraft

At the outbreak of war, as described above, all aviation units were subordinated to individual army commands, leaving none available for wider strategic objectives. This weakness was overcome in April 1915 by the creation of a formation code-named Carrier Pigeon Unit Ostend (Brieftauben-Abteilung Ostende, BAO), which was quickly joined by a second unit, BA Metz (BAM). These two units came under the direct command of OHL, which was able to use them as a strategic bombing reserve for both Western and Eastern fronts.

Navy Zeppelin L59 emerges from its shed at Staaken. L59 mounted the bold 'Africa Raid' of November 1917, setting off from Bulgaria loaded with food, ammunition and medical supplies for Lettow-Vorbeck's forces in East Africa. It had got as far as the Sudan when it was recalled, in the mistaken belief that Lettow-Vorbeck had been captured. (IWM Q58475)

To make it easier to move along the front, each of the two units was based around a train, which ferried aircraft, crews and equipment wherever the situation dictated. Two dining cars served as a mess (Kasino), and some Belgian Railways sleeping cars were fitted out for the aircrews. The train would deliver the crews to the airfield early in the morning, and collect them again at night – a facility that was much appreciated by the men. Oberleutnant Carganico remembered: 'When you sat there, you really felt cosy, as if you were sat in a room in a doll's house. When you returned from a flight, there was always a place of quiet comfort to rest... Even if we travelled by air [to another part of the front] our living quarters rolled after us, and were ready for us in the evening.'

To ensure complete independence in its operations, the BAO even carried its own wooden runway, which could be taken off the train, laid down and assembled in just a few days. Its aircraft, disassembled for transport by train, were sheltered in large canvas tents at their new airfield. These tents were standard throughout the Air Service: made by Baumann & Lederer of Kassel, they could each accommodate two two-seaters.

Since OHL assembled the best pilots and observers for the two units, they were an immediate success, and more were formed. Renamed Kampfgeschwäder der Obersten Heeresleitung (Kagohl), their number rose briefly to seven by early 1916, before four were disbanded in the summer of the same year. Each Kagohl was composed of a number of Kampfstaffeln (Kasta) of six aircraft. Originally these were the same Albatros CIIIs that equipped many of the FFAs, but over the winter of 1915–16 the Kasta were re-equipped with AEG G-Types, which were better suited to their task. Each of these aircraft had a crew of three (pilot, observer and gunner); a ground crew of 100 men supported them, with additional officers and men acting as the Geschwader staff.

Despite their elite status and their function as a strategic bomber reserve, the Kagohl still found themselves drawn into the air superiority

An AEG GIII bomber of Kagohl I preparing for take-off in Macedonia during 1916. The pilot has retained his early padded helmet, while the gunner prefers a lighter leather item. Although the 'Giant' R-Types carried twice as many, the crew of a G-Type bomber was only three, with the gunner manning several different mountings. The pilot was often not the aircraft commander; the latter performed the duties of navigator and bomb aimer. (IWM Q54441)

battles over Verdun and the Somme in 1916, to the detriment of their specialist role. In summer 1917 a change of priorities by Kogenluft saw many Kasta converted into Schlasta. The remainder were reorganized into three Bombengeschwäder der OHL (Bogohl); two of these comprised three Staffeln (Bosta) each, but Bogohl 3 was larger with six flights. Each Bosta consisted originally of three G-Types – either AEGs, Friedrichshafens or Gothas. This number was increased to eight in 1918, with an additional six to eight Rumpler or DFW C-Types for daylight operations. The staff of Bogohl 3 consisted of a commanding officer, an adjutant, intelligence, meteorological, photo-graphic, transport and technical officers, with clerical support, and around 120 mechanics.

Of all the bomber Geschwäder, the most famous was Kagohl/Bogohl 3, equipped with Gotha GIVs and initially led by the charismatic Hptm Ernst Brandenburg, which was tasked with bombing strategic targets in England. Between 25 May 1917 and 20 May 1918, bombers based around Ghent raided London and the South Coast on 27 different occasions. The first eight of these raids were made in daylight, but improvements in the British defences later forced a switch to night operations. Although the bomber units took few losses in aerial combat, they did suffer steady attrition from technical failures and landing accidents; and after Hptm Brandenburg (who received the Pour le Mérite following the London raid of 13 June 1917) was injured in an accident and relinquished command, the morale of Kagohl 3 is said to have suffered.

The difficulties of mounting raids that crossed the Allied lines, particularly in daylight, meant that a distant target like Paris saw only 30 attacks during the whole of the war, with most of the bombs falling around the rail yards in the northern suburb of La Villette. Long range raids reduced the bombload of the Gotha GIV to about 660lb instead of the theoretical 1,100lb; most attacks were directed against targets closer to the front, such as the Channel ports (especially Dunkirk) and the important French airfield at St Pol.

During combat, fighter aircraft often lost formation to engage in individual duels with the enemy. In contrast, the bombers, flying at around 10,000–12,000ft, stayed strictly in formation, both to and from the target area, enabling them to use their defensive firepower to the maximum. On reaching the target the Kagohl sometimes attacked in one wave, but usually it was considered to be more effective to go in Staffel by Staffel at timed intervals. This staged form of attack, designed to exhaust the enemy defences, could last for up to five hours. In the summer of 1918 a new tactic was introduced: a number of two-seaters preceded the attack as pathfinders, and dropped flares to illuminate potential targets.

An observer in the basket of a tethered balloon, with his *Flieger Kammer III* camera. Such cameras, with their long focal length (in this case 70cm), were able to capture detailed images of the Allied front lines. However, the oblique angle at which the pictures were taken resulted in distortions of scale that could only be corrected by overhead photography from an aircraft. (IWM Q23905)

The Bosta (and the Reihenbildner photo-reconnaissance aircraft) flew at such heights that shortage of oxygen could present a problem to their crews. Oxygen sets were fitted in some aircraft and filled with liquid oxygen just before take off. As the internal pressure of the tank increased with altitude, a safety valve was needed; but this in its turn reduced the amount of available oxygen. The problem was solved by the introduction of a barometric valve, which automatically regulated the flow of oxygen according to the altitude.

The ineffectiveness of the airship as a bomber prompted the Germans to develop a new long range aircraft as a replacement. Inspired by the Russian Sikorski Ilya Mourometz bomber, the result was the 'Giant' Zeppelin-Staaken RIV and RVI (with six engines, the RIV had a wingspan of more than 138ft – only 33in less than that of the B-29 Superfortress). In January 1916 the first unit to be equipped with these types, Riesenflugzeug Abteilung 500, was formed, to be followed by three more numbered 501 to 503 during the course of the year. The four units served on the Eastern Front until September 1917; then, merged into two, they were moved to the West. Each unit was as self-contained as possible, with a wide range of specialist mechanics and engineers, and even its own meteorological officer – in total some 20 officers and around 750 men. Although the Giants had a flight endurance of up to eight hours, and carried a much larger load than the Gothas of Kagohl 3 – 2,600lb over long distances, and up to 5,000lb for shorter flights – they frequently suffered technical problems, and were able to undertake only a few missions during the winter of 1917–18 before they were diverted to support the March 1918 offensive. In the face of the subsequent Allied advance, raids by Gothas and Giants were suspended completely. Altogether, 43 Gothas and 3 Giants were lost from a total of 413 sorties.

The benefits achieved for Germany by these bombing raids, whether by airship or aircraft, were extremely limited in terms of the eventual outcome of the war. Paradoxically, however, for Britain the long term results were extremely valuable. The raids on British cities had a significant effect on civilian morale, grossly out of proportion to the actual damage and casualties caused, and the press clamoured for effective counter-measures. The need for an air home defence system quickly forced the British government to reconsider the whole question of the command and control of the air forces. In the short term the raids obliged them to withdraw squadrons from the Western Front for home defence; in the long term, they were instrumental in the amalgamation of the RFC and RNAS as the unified Royal Air

A balloon loads up with a camera before ascending. Balloon troops continued to wear the Air Service shako until 1917, long after it had been withdrawn from the aircraft units. The pack of the Paulus parachute can just be seen hanging above the observer's head. (IWM Q53003)

Force in April 1918. The first steps taken in the planning of a co-ordinated system of raid reporting, AA defences, and the control of interceptor aircraft led directly to Britain's defensive success in 1940. The concept of the strategic air offensive would also colour post-war RAF thinking, and would lead eventually to the massive raids on Germany during World War II. In contrast, many senior Luftwaffe officers persisted in seeing these units purely as a tactical asset, and no successful long-range bomber would be developed under the Third Reich.

OBSERVATION BALLOONS

On mobilization, a tethered balloon section was attached to each army HQ. Each section consisted of one 600cc Parseval-Sigsfeld balloon, 4 observer officers, 177 enlisted ranks, 123 horses, 12 gas wagons, 2 equipment wagons, a winch wagon and a telephone wagon. A reserve gas column contained a further 12 gas wagons and an equipment wagon. The balloon had a theoretical ceiling of about 2,600ft, but in a strong breeze might reach only 1,600 feet. From 1915 onwards, these were replaced by balloons with a larger capacity of 800cc or 1,000cc, and with an increased ceiling of 3,000–3,500 feet. In good weather conditions, this allowed the observer a visual range of around 3½ miles into Allied lines. In 1916 a new type of balloon was introduced, the Caquot-type AE, based on a captured Allied design. This new model was stable in winds of up to 55mph and greatly improved the operational scope of the balloon.

At the beginning of the war a number of man-lifting kites were also available. In theory, these could be used when wind speeds prevented the safe use of a tethered balloon; a series of 12 kites could raise an observer to around 1,000 feet. However, in strong winds the kites proved to be of little more value than the more conventional balloons, and were rarely if ever employed.

For much of the war, each balloon section was independent, but this proved unwieldy in practice and led to much duplication of effort. To improve the dissemination of information from observers during the battle of Verdun, each army HQ formed a Ballonzentrale to collate all the data collected by its balloons. The distribution of balloon units was also reorganized. In March 1917, numbered balloon commands (1–45 Prussian and 61–68 Bavarian) were set up at each army HQ, and assigned a number of sections that varied with the tactical situation. The practical effect was that at least one balloon section was attached

Moving a kite balloon. Over short distances it was easier to 'walk' a balloon than to deflate it completely and then reflate it at its new location. Most balloon emplacements consisted of two 'beds', one of which acted as a reserve. (IWM Q54462)

to each division. Soon 135 numbered sections were in service (1–112 Prussian, 201–223 Bavarian), and this would rise to 182 by the end of the war. Each army HQ also formed a workshop and, from 1918, a mobile gas-generating unit that was transported by railway. Each army group contained an airship park, which provided replacement equipment, balloons and gas. Peace in the East following the collapse of Russia in 1917 enabled a park of this type to be set up in each army the following year.

Balloons were used primarily for artillery spotting and limited tactical reconnaissance; the balloons attached to corps HQs were used for observation and heavy artillery ranging, while those attached to divisions worked with both the infantry and the artillery. On each divisional front one balloon, known as an 'infantry balloon', served as the divisional observation post, maintaining a general watch on the front line. The role of the 'artillery balloon' was the observation of fire, principally German, but also flash spotting. Observing for flat trajectory super-heavy artillery needed two balloons, one on the line of fire for direction, and another to one side for range. During battle, another balloon might be launched to observe and report on fleeting targets of opportunity.

All balloons were equipped with telephones and with panoramic cameras. The telephones were connected to the appropriate artillery battery and to the Ballonzentrale, so that information could be collated and distributed easily. Communication between the observer and the front line units was also maintained by flare or lamp. For specific operations, each balloon flew a number of streamers below its basket as identification.

The importance of the role played by balloons in artillery spotting was noticed at Verdun by the French, who took special measures against them using aircraft armed with incendiary rockets. Their increased size and height meant that man- or even horse-powered winches could no longer lower them quickly and safely to the ground, particularly when they were under attack, and so motor winches were introduced. In 1915–16 observers were armed with a carbine for self-defence, but this was largely ineffectual against fast-moving aircraft, and it was abandoned in favour of improved anti-aircraft weapons on the ground.

Balloon observers were left to rely on their parachutes. The Paulus parachute, named after its inventor, was stowed in a pack attached to the rigging above the balloon basket, with two suspension lines which the observer snap-hooked to his harness before jumping. Jumping out of the basket ripped open the pack, detaching the parachute and allowing it to deploy. The parachute had several weak points, revealed by the stresses imposed by the jump, and a number of men fell to their deaths as a result: the cloth of the canopy might tear if it did not detach from its pack properly (which involved the snapping of a light cord at its apex), or the harness might fail. Nevertheless, parachute escapes from balloons were frequent: Vfw Stollwerck of Ballonzug 96 had made five jumps by July 1918, while the unlucky Lt Höfinghoff of Ballonzug 152 was forced to use his parachute three times in one 24-hour period on 15 September 1918.

Training for balloon observers was undertaken initially at Jüterbog, the home of the Army's artillery school. The balloon school was transferred to Namur in Belgium during the winter of 1916/17.

ANTI-AIRCRAFT DEFENCE

Ballonabwehrkanone & Fliegerabwehrkanone
In 1914 only 18 guns in the whole German Army were designated as anti-balloon weapons (Ballonabwehrkanone – Bak), and none as anti-aircraft weapons (Fliegerabwehrkanone – Flak). Of these, one motorized vehicle was attached to each of I, VIII and XXI Army Corps, and two to XV Corps. The remaining horse-drawn guns were assigned to protect strategically important locations along the axis of advance in the West.

After the outbreak of hostilities individual weapons were consolidated into sections, and then into platoons and batteries. Although their personnel were drawn from field artillery regiments, fixed and motorized Bak batteries came under the direct control of the army

A stereoscopic rangefinder in use by a Flak battery. Since the distance between the eyepiece and the lenses was known, and the angle they created when focusing on the target could be measured, it was a simple matter of geometry to work out the range. (IWM Q44802)

A battery of towed 90mm anti-aircraft guns on the Somme front. The gunners wear either shirtsleeves or the *Drillichanzug* fatigue uniform. In the right background, note men with a rangefinder and binoculars. (IWM Q44156)

commander via a specialist staff officer (Stabsoffizier der Bak – Stobak). The horse-drawn weapons, however, came under the control of divisional commanders.

Batteries of four guns, equipped with heavy 90mm or 100mm weapons, were placed to cover strategic targets. The divisional troops were equipped with 77mm field guns, or captured French 75s, mounted on locally made elevated mounts. Some sections, however, were equipped differently, employing either machine guns, or 37mm quick-firers obtained from the Navy, whose fire using tracer ammunition was known by the pilots of the RFC as 'flaming onions'.

Few Allied dirigible balloons took to the skies over the front, and in May 1916 Bak was renamed Fliegerabwehrkanone to represent its role more accurately (each Stobak thus became a Stoflak). At this time, there were 173 mobile and 2 fixed batteries; 16 motorized batteries; 217 mobile and 122 fixed platoons; and 14 motorized platoons. In December 1916 anti-aircraft troops were brought under the command of the Air Service, in order to improve co-operation; each Stoflak was redesignated Koflak (Flak commander), and a network of Group Flak Commanders (Flakgruko) were placed under him at divisional level. Flak artillery was now responsible not only for denying aerial reconnaissance and artillery spotting to the enemy, but also for supporting German aircraft in aerial combat. This was achieved partly through increasing the number of pivot-mounted weapons and placing them nearer the front line, and partly through the work of the aircraft reporting service.

All Flak units included listening equipment to aid in the speedy identification of approaching aircraft – an activity that was quickly expanded into the front lines. The listening posts of the aircraft reporting service reported all enemy aerial activity to the local

A well-camouflaged 77mm field gun employed in the AA role, mounted on a massive, specially built wheeled frame to greatly increase the elevation. (IWM Q57514)

(continued on page 41)

SERVICE DRESS, 1914–16
1: *Leutnant, Flieger Btl Nr.2;* Germany, July 1914
2: *Gemeine,* Bavarian *FFA 2;* Germany, c.June 1914
3: *Feldwebel* pilot, *FA 62;* France, 1916

1

2

3

A

FLYING CLOTHING & GROUND CREW WORKING DRESS
1: Pilot, 1914
2: *Hauptmann* Oswald Boelcke, *Jasta 2;* France, 1916
3: Ground crew

FLYING CLOTHING
1: Aircraft crew, 1915
2: NCO aircraft crew, 1916
3: Aircraft crew, 1917

C

FIGHTER PILOTS
1: *Rtm* Manfred Freiherr von Richthofen, *Jasta 11,* 1917
2: *Lt* Walter von Bülow-Bothkamp, *Jasta 36;* France, 1917
3: *Hptm* Hans-Joachim Buddecke, *FA 5;* Turkey, 1917

D

AIRSHIPS, BALLOONS & HIGH ALTITUDE AIRCRAFT
1: *Steuermann, Luftschiffer Abt Nr.1;* Germany, 1915
2: *Lt der R* Peter Rieper, *Ballonzug 19;* France, 1917–18
3: R-Type aircraft crew, 1917

1

2

3

E

AIRCREW, 1918
1: *Hptm* Eduard Ritter von Schleich, France
2: Ground attack aircraft crew, France
3: Pilot, *Jasta 300,* Palestine

F

SUPPORT SERVICES
1: *Flugmeldedienst,* France, 1917
2: Machine gunner of a *Flamga;* France, 1918
3: Meteorologist, Army Weather Service; France, 1916

NAVAL PERSONNEL
1: *Oblt der Matrosenartillerie* Friedrich Christiansen; Zeebrugge, 1917
2: *ObltzS* Theodor Osterkamp; Flanders, 1918
3: *Flugobermaat,* Naval Air Service; Flanders, 1916

H

Flakgruko at division HQ. From here, the report was channelled to the Koflak, who then passed it on to all the Flak units under his command, both at the front and in the rear areas, particularly those in the projected flight path of the enemy. The report was then also passed on to locally-based Jasta who might attempt interception. The listening posts were manned by an officer, two NCOs and four men, equipped with two theodolites, two telescopes, and a field telephone connection to their headquarters.

By 1918 the anti-aircraft establishment had increased considerably: it now comprised 116 heavy motorized batteries of two to three guns each; 39 light motorized batteries with two guns each; 168 horse-drawn batteries; 166 fixed batteries; 3 railway batteries; 183 quick-firer detachments; 49 horse-drawn detachments; 163 fixed detachments; and a further 80 motor Flak vehicles. Although guns of a variety of calibres were used, the heavy 90mm gun (542 weapons) and the lighter 37mm (196 weapons) predominated. Plans were made to standardize on an 88mm gun in 1918, but production could not keep pace with demand.

When machine guns were introduced in the anti-aircraft role they were not distributed among existing batteries but were formed instead into separate units – Fliegerabwehr Maschinengewehr Abteilungen (Flamga). The first Flamga were set up in August 1917, protecting industrial plants in Germany, and their number would eventually reach 103 units. On the Western Front, Flamga 801, 803, 901–921 and 925 were created to protect headquarters, munitions depots and other strategic centres just behind the front. Each Flamga consisted of three companies, each with 12 guns.

Searchlight sections, although they co-operated with the Flak, were originally independent of it, and were manned by troops from the Pioneers. In 1914 each active army corps, plus the Guard Reserve Corps, included a searchlight section, as did each siege train (an integral part of each Pioneer regiment). Each section comprised two officers and 39 men, responsible for one carriage-mounted and four portable lights. In early 1917 those sections on anti-aircraft duties

A battery of captured French Hotchkiss machine guns mounted on jury-rigged wheel mounts for the AA role. (IWM Q57521)

were attached to the anti-aircraft artillery, and were placed under the command of Kogenluft; 321 detachments were quickly formed, followed by a further 69 in 1918. From February 1918, these were combined into 87 'batteries' of three detachments each, leaving 129 independent detachments.

However alarming 'flaming onions' seemed to Allied pilots, the early effect of anti-aircraft fire on the enemy was negligible – in 1914 it took 11,500 rounds to shoot down one Allied plane. However, organizational and technical developments greatly enhanced its effectiveness. Bringing Flak and searchlight units under the command of the Air Service created a more integrated approach. The introduction of an improved stereoscopic rangefinder and mechanically timed fuses also helped to increase efficiency, as did the introduction of a fire director, although few had reached the front by the end of the war. By 1918 it took only 5,040 rounds – half the quantity needed during the first year of war – to shoot down an Allied aircraft. Overall, 748 aircraft were claimed by Flak units during the course of the war.

Flak training was undertaken within each artillery regiment, although a live firing school was also set up at Ostend, with a range at Blankenberghe on the Belgian coast. A special school for motorized units was established in 1917 at Valenciennes. Searchlight training was undertaken at the school at Hannover created in December 1916, while training in direction-finding took place at La Fère (1915–17) or Ghent (1917–18).

Home defence units

The possibility of enemy air raids had been considered before war began, with plans for the creation of eight Fortress Flying Units (Festungsflieger Abteilungen), each equipped with four aircraft and intended to protect the area immediately surrounding fortress cities of strategic value. In fact, on mobilization 17 such units were created, each with six aircraft. By the end of the year, however, the progress of the conflict suggested that these valuable assets were better employed in front line formations. The fortress units were all converted into FFAs to serve at the front, leaving little to counter any aerial threat to Germany. Individual army corps areas had a number of Flak batteries, and individual single-seater aircraft, but these formed part of no overall co-ordinated organization.

This unsatisfactory state of affairs was remedied in December 1916 by the creation of a new post, Commander of Home Air Defence (Koluftheim), who was responsible for the air defence of German territory, and who reported directly to Kogenluft. To protect factories and airfields, Kogenluft eventually had at his disposal 11 fighter Kampfeinsitzerstaffeln (Kesta – renamed Jasta in October 1918); ten Flak groups covering the western frontier, 103 machine gun detachments, nine barrage balloon sections, and the aircraft reporting service, all connected by a wireless network. The Kesta – typically a mixture of pilots straight from training schools and veterans in need of a rest from the front – achieved little against enemy raids, with only 36 confirmed victories over a period of two years. Many more Allied aircraft fell to front line Jasta and Flak as the bombers passed over the front lines.

COMMAND, TRAINING & SUPPORT

Higher command

The increasing importance of aviation in the minds of the German High Command was reflected by the creation in 1913 of separate Airship and Aviation Inspectorates (Ilust and Idflieg) within the Communications Inspectorate. The two inspectors were responsible only for equipping and arming units, but not for their operating doctrine or their tactical employment. However, motivated by a distrust of what it saw as too much Prussian influence in the armed forces, the Kingdom of Bavaria insisted on maintaining its own establishment, responsible for manning and, initially, for procurement as well. Although all the flying units in the German Army were numbered in one sequence, Bavarian units, designated by the 'b' suffix, were the responsibility of their own Inspectorate, Iluk, and not Idflieg. Bavarian units were uniformed according to their own regulations, and equipped as much as possible with Bavarian-made aircraft – the Otto pusher, the Pfalzes and license-built Rolands. As the war progressed, however, this independence was increasingly difficult to maintain in the face of the desire of the Imperial authorities to standardize equipment within the Air Service.

With the early failure of the airship as a tactical weapon, many of the missions envisaged for them were allocated instead to aircraft, increasing the importance of the new arm. Experience in the field during the opening months of the war also showed that changes were needed in the command structure. In March 1915, therefore, a new post was created, Chef des Feldflugwesens (Feldflugchef), in command of all aviation units in the field and at home, whether lighter or heavier than air; he was also responsible for the Aviation Inspectorate, and thus for aircraft production. This, it was hoped, would provide a unified direction to the Air Service. The new post was given to Maj Hermann Thomsen (later von der Lieth-Thomsen), an officer who had served on the General Staff, and had acted as an advisor on military aeronautics before the outbreak of war.

Thomsen was an inspired appointment. General Falkenhayn later commented that the new man 'not only understood how to direct aircraft production at home along the right lines, but also how to keep up the true aviator's spirit among the men, without which all technical skills would have meant nothing'. Co-operation with the Inspector, Maj (later Obstlt) Siegert, was also vital, and fortunately Siegert was of a similar mind to Thomsen. A contemporary wrote that Siegert's 'ebullient spirit and his imagination, which seemed almost utopian, was often misunderstood. But he anticipated developments by many years and was always productive. To Major Siegert, as well as to the steely but sober organizer Major

GenLt Ernst von Höppner, *Kogenluft* (left). Höppner was a cavalryman who had begun the war as chief-of-staff to 3.Armee. After a period leading 17.Division, then as chief-of-staff of 2.Armee, he was transferred from the command of 75.Reserve Division to his new post as commanding general of the Air Service. The pilot he is speaking to wears a typically non-regulation combination of flying garments: an issue padded helmet, a private purchase scarf, a three-quarter length greatcoat worn over a flying suit, and ankle boots. (IWM Q56576)

Table 7: KOFL staff, 1918

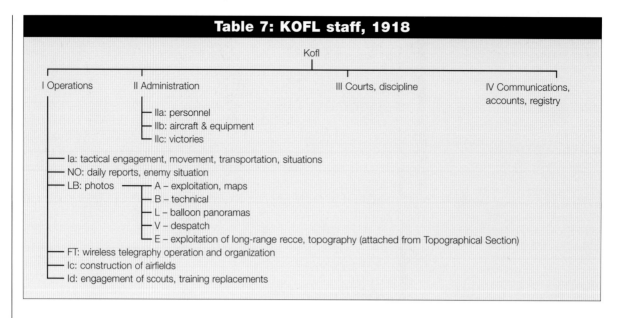

```
                                          Kofl
        ┌──────────────┬───────────────────┴───────────┬──────────────────────┐
   I Operations    II Administration             III Courts, discipline    IV Communications,
                                                                            accounts, registry
                        ├── IIa: personnel
                        ├── IIb: aircraft & equipment
                        └── IIc: victories
    ├── Ia: tactical engagement, movement, transportation, situations
    ├── NO: daily reports, enemy situation
    ├── LB: photos ──┬── A – exploitation, maps
    │                ├── B – technical
    │                ├── L – balloon panoramas
    │                ├── V – despatch
    │                └── E – exploitation of long-range recce, topography (attached from Topographical Section)
    ├── FT: wireless telegraphy operation and organization
    ├── Ic: construction of airfields
    └── Id: engagement of scouts, training replacements
```

Thomsen, aviation troops owe their massive scale of development. It was unique in the history of the German Army.'

In October 1916, Gen Hindenburg set in motion a further reorganization of the Air Service. As originally developed by Thomsen, the plans called for all aviation services, Army and Navy, to be unified under a single authority. This never happened, since the Naval Staff refused to co-operate with the scheme; but the Army's Air Service did expand, taking over responsibility for Flak and for the meteorological service. The size and importance of the expanded Air Service demanded a new command structure, led by an active commander reporting direct to the General Staff. The man chosen to fill this new post of Kommandierender General der Luftstreitkräfte (Kogenluft) was a cavalryman, GenLt Ernst von Höppner, with Thomsen as his chief-of-staff.

For the front line units the reorganization brought immediate benefits, facilitating communication between previously independent elements of the Army. However, in 1917 Kogenluft also faced the challenge of American entry into the war. His response was an unprecedented expansion of the Air Service – the 'Amerikaprogram'. Based on the correct assumption that the full impact of American intervention would not be felt until the following year, the plan was launched in the early summer of 1917. It called for the establishment of 40 new Jasta, 17 FAA, one Kagohl and two Schlasta; for existing flying schools to be expanded and another created; for engine production to increase from 2,000 to 2,500 per month, and aircraft production to be doubled to 2,000 machines per month; for oil and fuel allocations to the Air Service to be increased, and for a further 24,000 men to be recruited. All this had to be in place by 1 March 1918.

Table 8: IDFLIEG staff, 1918

Flugzeugmeisterei:
  Abteilung für Konstruktions Neuheiten (Konab) *new inventions*
  Prüfanstalt und Werft (PuW) *testing*
  Zentral Abnahme Kommission (ZAK) *acceptance*
  Licht u. Bild Abteilung (Lubia) *photo-recce equipment supply*
  Waffen u. Munitions Beschaffungsamt (Wumba) *ordnance supply*
  Fabrikaufsicht *factories inspectorate*
  Motoren Abteilung *engines inspectorate*

Kommando der Flieger Ersatz Abteilungen (KdoFea) *training units*
Kommando der Riesenflugzeug Abteilungen (Kdo Rfla) *R-Type units*
Hauptkassenverwaltung *home formations & establishments*
Bekleidungsamt *clothing*
Sonderbekleidungsamt *flying clothing*

Given the conditions prevailing in Germany at this period of the war the plan was over-ambitious, and it is hardly surprising that it failed in most respects. A shortage of raw materials meant that the aircraft industry had no chance of even approaching its targets. The new Jasta were created, but only at the cost of cutting training schedules and leaving many existing units understrength in terms of aircraft and experienced personnel. The problems thus caused were only exacerbated by further losses in men and aircraft when the poorly trained pilots reached the front.

The loss of officers had already begun to bite, and suitable candidates for flying training were sought throughout the Army. In June 1917 all units, but especially cavalry units, were encouraged to send in lists of suitable candidates, and a month later lines-of-communications units were also combed out. Even these measures failed to produce the numbers required, and in June 1918 candidates were sought once more from other arms of service. Front line regiments had already lost skilled personnel to specialist units in 1917, and were very reluctant to lose more. Indeed, ground crews, far from recruiting new men, were being combed out hungrily to fill gaps in the infantry. A further, almost irrelevant complication was the insistence of the King of Baden that Badeners should, at this late stage, form their own units.

Training

Aircrew were drawn from the ranks of officers and NCOs. However, the usual practice in two-seater units, particularly in the first years of the war, was for officers to take the position of observer and for NCOs to act as pilots. It was argued that only an officer could appreciate the dispositions of the enemy troops he saw below, and observers were certainly expected to help in evaluating the photographs they had taken. Schröder thought that officer observers were drawn from those who were interested in strategy and tactics, and not in sport – in contrast to the RFC, where officer pilots were the norm. Nevertheless, the practice does carry overtones of officers being 'chauffeured' by enlisted ranks. Basing their assessment on the interrogation of captured aircrew from Bogohl 3, British intelligence suggested that there was some friction between NCOs and officers, but were unable to pin down the exact cause.

Air Service officers, like their opponents, might either belong to the flying troops *ab initio*, or be transferred in from other arms. The first training school for officers who volunteered as pilots opened at Döberitz on 4 July 1910, but local restrictions limited the amount of flying that could take place, and the establishment soon became inadequate for the numbers involved. Aircraft manufacturers, such as Albatros and Gotha, were asked to fill the breach and set up training schools at their factories, and two further Army flying schools were opened at Strasburg in Alsace and Metz in Lorraine. From March 1915 a school was also attached to each replacement unit (Flieger Ersatz Abteilung); 14 were created on the Prussian establishment and two on the Bavarian, gradually replacing those of the manufacturers.

The Ersatz Abteilung was divided into five companies. Basic training was undertaken in the Recruit Company (Rekrutenkompanie). Those already in the Army were sent to the Conversion Unit (Vorratsschule)

Fokker triplanes of Jasta 12 are wheeled out of their tented hangars at Marle, north of Laon, for a patrol over the Chemin des Dames, scene of the disastrous French 'Nivelle Offensive' of April 1917. The triplane was light and highly manoeuvrable, with a phenomenal rate of climb, although it was not as fast as some Allied types. Initially it suffered from structural failures due to poor factory quality control, which reduced its use at the front. (IWM Q63142)

for four to 12 weeks, before passing on to the Flying Company (Fliegerkompanie) or to a manufacturer's school for flight training. Trainee mechanics were directed to the Werftkompanie, while the fifth company provided men for fatigue parties, guards and other general duties. The aircraft used by the training units were obsolete, since most of the latest models went to the front. Hans Schröder recalled his training days in December 1915: 'The aircraft park at Böblingen was a miserable affair, for there was nothing but some old Eulers, the two Aviatiks and one new AEG fighter... The old ones were good enough for the pupils, and no protests availed as long as these honourable buses were safe to fly.'

The pilot's examination was in three stages. The first part was similar to the exam for civilian pilots and consisted of flying a series of figures-of-eight, covering a total distance of 5km (3 miles). Even famous flyers like Richthofen and Boelcke found it difficult to pass this initial stage. The second required the pilot to complete a cross-country flight, one hour in length. The third element, introduced in 1915, included flights over the front line. As the war progressed, changes were introduced: in January 1916 the exam requirements were tightened up to take account of conditions at the front; then, as units had begun to specialize, pilot training did likewise, with extra courses for pilots of C- and G-Types, as well as for the single-seater D-Types. The new syllabus included landings, from level and from spiralling flight, a high altitude flight, and a 60km (37 mile) cross-country flight.

The instructors at the manufacturers' schools had their pay docked if any of their pupils failed to pass – hardly an incentive to turn out properly qualified personnel. Even so, British intelligence estimated that half of all German candidates failed to pass their flight training.

The interior of an aircraft repair shop, possibly at an airfield but more likely at an army aircraft park. The machines are Albatros B-Types.

A quarter of the whole were killed in crashes during basic training, and a small number during advanced training, while another quarter failed due to ill-health, undesirable conduct or problems of morale. Statistics published by the Reichsarchiv in 1924–25 show 3,496 casualties as a result of flying accidents in Germany during the war, from a total of 16,054 Air Service losses from all causes.

For most new pilots, the next step was a move to an army aircraft park to wait for a vacancy in an operational unit. This posting would normally last from one to three months, although in periods of heavy fighting it could be reduced to as little as a fortnight.

Simply by the nature of the Air Service's equipment, most single-seater pilots before 1917–18 had seen some initial service with two-seater units, and transferred only at their own request. Only the best of the successful candidates would be considered for training as single-seater pilots. These lucky few went first to Mannheim to familiarize themselves with flying single-seaters, and then to one of three Jasta Schools to learn combat formation flying under the eyes of experienced pilots. Such expert instruction was of critical importance, and from March 1917 completion of these courses was made obligatory for all Jasta pilots. Yet only one month later, pilot shortages – the result of the Amerikaprogram – had forced the closure of the Mannheim establishment and two of the three Jasta Schools. Instead, training was completed within the Jasta, even if this meant sending the unit to the rear for a time. The results were unsurprising: a large increase in the number of poorly trained pilots, and a consequent rise in the number of casualties.

No specialist training facility was provided for bomber pilots until April 1916, when a school for those flying R-Types was opened at Döberitz, before the flying training element moved to Cologne at the end of 1917.

Observers came initially from the ranks of qualified pilots, but later non-pilots were also trained for this role. Observers underwent a six-week basic training course at an Ersatz Abteilung, before those intended for bomber units went on to the Bombenlehr Kommando, the specialist school in Frankfurt an der Oder. Those destined for artillery units attended the Artillerie Fliegerschule at Jüterbog, followed by an air gunnery course at Asch, Belgium. A new school for observers was set up at Königsberg in 1916, but it was soon divided into two sections, located at Jüterbog and Großenhain. Each school dealt with around 50 trainees at any one time.

Some mechanics received their training simply by working alongside a fully trained colleague, but ideally they attended the Werftkompanie of a Flieger Ersatz Abteilung. These provided courses in general maintenance, as well as specialist classes for riggers, splicers and welders. Engine mechanics were sent to train with one of the manufacturers – Maybach, Benz, Oberursel, Argus, Mercedes or Bosch – with the consequent disadvantage that their expertise was limited only to that make of engine.

Support services

Most aviation, airship and balloon units included a number of men taken straight from civilian life and employed solely for their technical qualifications. Although they wore uniform, they did not have any command responsibilities.

The aircraft of Jasta 12, a mixture of Albatros DIIIs and Fokker DrIs, lined up at Toulis airfield near Laon. The squadron buildings, such as they are, are located near the road junction in the background. Life was spartan for most front line flying units. (IWM Q23907)

On mobilization, each FFA, Park and Ersatz Abteilung received two Equipment Officers (Werkmeister); each airship battalion contained a workshop manager (Werkstättenvorsteher), two or three hangar inspectors (Luftschiffhalleninspekteure) and a parts controller (Materialverwalter). As the war progressed their numbers multiplied. By 1918 every front line aviation unit had two Werkmeister, and each replacement unit included four such men and an engineer. Each airship park, replacement unit and workshop included a machinist or hangar inspector. The Army trained its own Werkmeister through the Ersatz Abteilung and the Test Establishment of the Aircraft Inspectorate at Adlershof.

The Army Meteorological Service also included many such temporary officers, particularly amongst its specialist meteorologists. Although its headquarters were in Berlin, over the winter of 1914–15 it set up field headquarters at Brussels, Warsaw and Temesvar (transferred in 1916 to Sofia and Constantinople). Reporting to them was a series of weather stations (Armee Wetterwarte, Awewa) – 24 fixed and 27 mobile (one per army). In 1917 these were further augmented by 210 stations in the front line (Front Wetterwarte), and by 11 weather balloon detachments (Front Wetterdienstdrachenwarte, Fedrawa).

Airfields

These were frequently just what the name implies – a reasonably level meadow, placed close to a village or main road. Local civilians and their grazing animals were employed to keep the grass short. More care had to be taken in maintaining sites accommodating units equipped with Gothas and 'Giants'; these aircraft had such fragile undercarriages that the fields they used had to be rolled completely flat.

Securing quarters close by was something of a lottery; the men might find themselves billeted in a local farmhouse or its outbuildings, or even, if they were lucky, in a local château. If they were unlucky, then

A bleak view of Pontlaverger airfield, near Rheims, in July 1918; an Allied counter-offensive in this sector commenced on the 12th of that month. The aircraft, mostly Fokker DVIIs, await the order to take off, while crews take the opportunity to snatch a meal, seated among boxes and bed rolls. (IWM Q52996)

everyone lived under canvas; if they were very unlucky, like Schröder's FA 6 in Galicia, they had to fumigate a louse-ridden shack before they could move in. The crews of the seaplane flight based at Zeebrugge were accommodated in some style at the Grand Hotel, while their mechanics were billeted in local houses (the aircraft were housed in a railway station hall at the end of the Mole). Their comrades in II Torpedostaffel, also based at Zeebrugge in 1917, lived aboard a ship, the *Brügge*, moored in the harbour.

Aircraft were housed in Baumann u. Lederer tents on forward airfields or as a temporary measure. More permanent installations, both hangars and offices, were constructed by the Hallenbau companies (two Prussian and one Bavarian), created in 1916 and 1917 respectively.

THE NAVAL AIR SERVICE

In 1914 the German Naval Air Service was even smaller than that of the Army. The Navy expected that a British blockade would force the German fleet to fight close to its bases. Consequently, its airships, and particularly its aircraft, only had a short range, and their operational role was envisaged solely in terms of protecting the battle fleet. On the outbreak of war there were no more than 20 qualified pilots, and no observers; six seaplanes in the North Sea and three in the Baltic; and only one operational airship.

Nevertheless, the Navy insisted on setting up its own organization separate from that of the Army, and even in 1916 it fought off the Army's attempts to create a single command for all aviation elements in the armed forces. Since their two spheres of operations rarely overlapped, however, this had little effect on the conduct of operations.

Naval aviation was directed by the Navy Ministry, the Reichsmarineamt, and its commander was the Marineflugchef. The Naval Air Service had three depots: I.Seeflieger Abteilung (Kiel), which manned the seaplane bases in the Baltic, Kurland, the Adriatic and the Aegean; II.Seeflieger Abteilung (Wilhelmshaven), responsible for seaplane bases on North Sea coasts, including Zeebrugge and Ostend; and the Marine

Landflieger Abteilung (Johannisthal, near Berlin), responsible for all land bases at home, in Flanders or in the Balkans. A fourth depot, Marine Küstenflieger Abteilung, was created with special responsibility for the Belgian coastline. Its units, and those of the Marine Landflieger operating in Flanders, were grouped as Flieger der Marinekorps, with its HQ at Bruges. Airships were manned through two Marine Luftschiffer Abteilungen, Nord See and Ost See, responsible for the North Sea and the Baltic respectively.

Airship training took place originally at Fuhlsbüttel, near Hamburg, and Frankfurt am Main; but in 1914 it was moved to Leipzig, transferring to Dresden in 1915, and finally to Nordholz in the following year. Basic flying training was undertaken at one of these three depots. Before peace was declared with Russia in 1917, advanced training, including observer training, took place at the unit. With the arrival of peace in the East, however, advanced training moved instead to some of the Baltic bases.

Naval aviation comprised three main elements: airships (discussed above), seaplanes and land-based aircraft. For operations over water the Navy preferred seaplanes to flying boats, on the grounds of their greater stability on the rough waters of the North Sea. The seaplanes of the Seeflieger Abteilung primarily played an anti-shipping role – laying mines, and conducting operations against Allied warships, particularly submarines, which strayed into the seas off the Belgian and German coasts, and against merchant vessels off the British and French coasts. Their principal weapon was the bomb: they normally carried a stick of at least five 10kg (22lb) bombs, which had proved more effective at hitting the target than a smaller number of heavier bombs. Some work was undertaken with torpedo aircraft, and two Staffeln were based on the Belgian coast in 1916–17; but they proved ineffective, largely because the machines they employed were under-powered.

A group of naval aircrew pose in front of their Friedrichshafen FF33E seaplane. No two men wear exactly the same uniform. The pilot (left) wears a leather helmet and coat, with breeches, long socks, leather leggings and ankle boots; the warrant officer next to him wears his cap with its distinctive badge; the third man wears leather trousers with his *Jacke*, although neither he, nor the right-hand officer wearing a short overcoat, appear to be wearing aircrew badges. (IWM Q47973)

Other seaplanes were devoted to the interdiction of Allied aircraft. Like land-based fighters, they began by working alone but, influenced by Jasta tactics, they eventually came to operate in flights of three, five or even seven machines.

A flight of fighter aircraft, the Marine Feld Jagdstaffel, was formed at the end of 1916 to operate in Flanders in support of naval ground troops. This was later supplemented by four similar units – two more Marine Feld Jasta and two Seefrontstaffeln, formed for the defence of the Flanders coast. All five were formed into a Geschwader under Gotthard Sachsenberg in 1918. Four Küstenfliegerstaffeln (Kusta) were created in 1917 to perform spotting work with coastal batteries on the Belgian coast, followed by two Marine Schusta to protect them, all operating Albatros CVIIs, DFW CVs and LVG CVs. In 1918, following Air Service practice, the Schusta were converted to Schlasta, operating LVGs and Halberstadt CLIIs in a ground support role. A further flight, the Marine Sonderstaffel, was devoted to the defence of the U-boat installations at Bruges against raids by British Handley-Page bombers.

Naval flying training was divided into two paths, for land planes and seaplanes. The former was concentrated at Johannisthal, with an observer's school at Hage and a Jasta school at Danzig. The latter was split between sites along the German coast – including Wilhelmshaven (technical training), Kiel (pilots and mechanics), Danzig (single-seaters) and even as far as Finland.

The internal organization of naval units reflected their service origins. Each was split into three divisions: flying personnel, mechanics,

Navy pilots pose around a Friedrichshafen FF33L seaplane at Zeebrugge; again, all of them are dressed slightly differently. See under Plate H on page 63 for naval uniform practices. Two (third and fifth from left) wear field-grey, with shoulder boards and cuff rings respectively; the rest wear navy blue. Some wear puttees and others leggings; some a soft collar and tie, one man a wing collar and bow tie. The *Bootsmann* (centre rear) wears ratings' working dress. The 'civilian' official (second from left, foreground) is perhaps an engineer or a doctor, and wears distinctive velvet collar facing on his undress *Rock*. (IWM Q52994)

Returning a Friedrichshafen FF33L to its transportation trolley at a Belgian dockside. For ease of handling the engine is kept running, so that the aircraft always points into the wind. The 33L was the most numerous of the fighter variants of this series, an agile, seaworthy machine with a flight endurance of between five and six hours. (IWM Q54385)

and Starttruppen (i.e. guards, drivers and working parties); and each division was further divided into port and starboard watches, just as on a warship.

The Navy also established parallel Flak and balloon organizations. They maintained three Flak Gruppen at Bruges, Zeebrugge and Gistel; three balloon sections at Bredene, Gistel-Zevecote and Boverkerke-Kortewilde; and a searchlight troop, with an HQ at Knokke.

CONCLUSION

One of the most remarkable features of the Air Service during 1914–18 is the way it expanded from almost nothing to become a formidable instrument of war. In 1914 there were only some 500 men in the Air Service; by the end of the war there were 80,000, of whom 5,000 were flying personnel.

For the period between 1916 and September 1918, the Service claimed a total of 6,961 enemy aircraft destroyed, against the loss of 1,972 German machines. In addition, the Navy claimed in the region of 270 aircraft destroyed (as well as eight warships and four merchantmen) against around 170 losses. Figures produced in 1924–25 revealed the human cost. The Air Service lost a total of 18,372 men during the war (16,054 aircrew and 2,318 other personnel) – a figure which includes 7,850 lost in action and 5,207 in accidents at the front. The losses include 3,010 men who were reported missing: the statistics do not differentiate between prisoners – some of whom must have returned to Germany after the war – and those whose fate remains 'unknown'.

A Brandenburg W12 seaplane from Zeebrugge takes the opportunity to show off in front of some bathing belles on the beach at Ostend. The slab-sided appearance of this 1917 type was belied by its speed and manoeuvrability; in the hands of Oblt Christiansen's men from Zeebrugge it was a most capable opponent for British heavy flying boats. (IWM Q54387)

German aircraft manufacturers and designers were able to produce a succession of technically excellent types that gave the Germans air superiority on a number of occasions. However, contemporary technology had its limitations. Engines were insufficiently powerful and bombsights insufficiently accurate to support the strategic use of airpower. It was perhaps this above all that forced the Germans to view the Air Service purely as a tactical weapon. German attitudes to airpower were made plain by OHL in June 1918; 'Airmen', it explained, 'like other troops, should attack the enemy on the ground with the object of causing casualties and of breaking his morale.' Night bombing raids composed of several flights under one command, and including Giant groups, should attack railway junctions. Further attacks by individual two-seaters of the Bosta should be made on convoys and trains by night, and also by day where air supremacy permitted. Motor vehicles and troop columns were to be attacked methodically and continuously by Schlasta or Schlachtgruppen, especially in defiles, at crossroads or in villages. Fighters were also to be employed in this way, as were the Bosta two-seaters when not employed in night bombing.

Moreover, throughout the war the Service was hampered by the relatively small size of the aircraft industry and the effects of the Allied blockade. Both Feldflugchef and Kogenluft were well aware of the advantages of standardization of aircraft types within each unit – the Amerikaprogram called for all Jasta to be equipped with the Fokker DVII during 1919; yet the industry was never able to deliver aircraft in sufficient numbers to make this idea a reality, a state of affairs that only worsened as the war progressed. The Germans were obliged to make the most of their limited resources. The approach of Gen Ludendorff – effectively Chief of the General Staff from 1916 onwards – was to create commands built around function, rather than relying on the hierarchical pre-war chain of command. This is apparent in his 1916–17 reorganization of the Air Service; for example, in the way the Service took over Flak and searchlight defences.

In his volume of reminiscence, *Flying Fury*, the British ace Maj James McCudden wrote that

> The German aviator is disciplined, resolute and brave and is a foeman worthy of our best. Although I have seen some cases where a German aviator has on occasion been a coward yet I have seen on the other hand many incidents which have given me food for thought and have caused me to respect the German. The more I fight them the more I respect their fighting qualities. I have on many occasions had German machines at my mercy over the lines and they have had the choice of landing and being taken prisoner or being shot down. With one exception, they chose the latter path.

SELECT BIBLIOGRAPHY

Much modern writing on the German Air Service concerns the fighter aces, their aircraft and their victims, to the neglect of the remaining units. The most encyclopaedic of these is perhaps *Above the Lines: the Aces and Fighter Units of the German Air Service, Naval Air Service and Flanders Marine Corps 1914–1918* by Norman Franks, Frank Bailey & Russell Guest (London, 1995); while the career and fate of the Red Baron is an industry in itself. *Germany's First Air Force 1914–1918* by Peter Kilduff (London, 1991) attempts to redress the balance by concentrating on the two-seater and bomber crews. The bombing raids against England are covered in great detail by Ray Rimmell, *Zeppelin* (London, 1984) and by H.B. Castle, *Storm over England* (London, 1988). Despite its age, Alex Imrie's *Pictorial History of the German Army Air Service* (London, 1971) remains valuable, particularly on organization. In German, three works contain much useful information in personal accounts: *Unserere Luftstreitkräfte 1914–1918: ein Denkmal deutschen Heldentums*, edited by Walter von Eberhardt (Berlin, 1930); and Georg Neumann's two books, *Die deutschen Luftstreitkräfte im Weltkriege* (Berlin, 1920) and *In der Luft unbesiegt* (Munich, 1925). An English translation of the former was published in 1926 and was reprinted as recently as 2004, but it omits much material, particularly on organization. Hans Schröder's memoirs, *A German Airman Remembers*, were reprinted in 1986.

On the internet, the multilingual site *<www.frontflieger.de>* covers the units and the personnel of the Army Air Service in some detail. Another site *<www.jastaboelcke.de>* deals with both the great man and the unit named after him. In German, *<www.idflieg.de>* has much to offer on Air Service personnel, while *<luftschiff.krug77.de>* contains much valuable information on airships and their commanders. A purely English language site *<www.theaerodrome.com>* again concentrates on the aces, but has an exceptionally useful and informative forum, covering all aspects of the war in the air.

The two journals *Cross and Cockade* and *Over the Front* continue to provide thorough, well-researched articles on all aspects of World War I aviation.

GLOSSARY

b	*bayerisches* – suffix to unit number indicating Bavarian
Bogohl	*Bombengeschwader der Obersten Heeresleitung* – bomber unit organization that replaced the Kagohl (qv), divided into six Bosta (qv)
Bosta	*Bombenstaffel* – flight of six bombers
C	Designation for single-engine armed biplanes
D	Designation for single-engine, single-seat armed biplanes
Dr	Designation for triplanes
FA	*Flieger Abteilung* – basic aviation unit from Jan 1917, replacing FFA (qv)
FAA	*Flieger Abteilung (Artillerie)* – army co-operation unit
FAA Lb	*Flieger-Abteilung (Artillerie) mit Lichtbildgerät* – photo-reconnaissance unit
Feldflugchef	*Chef des Feldflugwesens* – officer responsible for equipping Air Service units, 1915–16
FFA	*Feldflieger Abteilung* – basic aviation unit, 1914–Dec 1916
FLA	*Feldluftschiffer Abteilung* – observation balloon unit
Flak	*Fliegerabwehrkanone* – anti-aircraft artillery
Flakgruko	*Gruppenkommandeur der Flak* – divisional AA commander
Flamga	*Fliegerabwehr Maschinengewehr Abteilung* – AA machine gun unit
G	Designation for multi-engined armed biplanes
Grufl	*Gruppenführer der Flieger* – senior air officer at an army corps HQ
Gruja	*Gruppenführer der Jagdgruppe* – commander of a *Jagdgruppe* (qv), the senior among the commanders of its component *Jagdstaffeln* (qv)
Idflieg	*Inspektion der Fliegertruppen* – Army aviation troops inspectorate
Iluft	*Inspektion der Luftschiffertruppen* – Army airship troops inspectorate
Iluk	*Inspektion des Militär Luft- und Kraftfahrwesens* – Bavarian equivalent of Idflieg (qv)
Jagdgeschwader (JG)	Permanent grouping of four *Jagdstaffeln*, introduced June 1917
Jagdgruppe	Temporary grouping of four *Jagdstaffeln*
Jasta	*Jagdstaffel* – basic fighter unit from August 1916, tactically divided into two *Schwarme*, each divided into two *Ketten* of two aircraft each
Kagohl	*Kampfgeschwader der Obersten Heeresleitung* – bomber/recce unit directly under OHL command, 1916, divided into six *Kampfstaffeln*; replaced by Bogohl (qv) in Oct 1917
Kasta	*Kampfstaffel* – flight of six bomber aircraft
KeK	*Kampfeinsitzer-Kommando* – single-seat fighter detachment, generally named after home airfield, e.g. Kek Metz
Kofl	*Kommandeur der Flieger* – commander of air units; replaced Stofl (qv)
Koflak	*Kommandeur der Flugabwehrkanone* – commander of AA troops at each army HQ
Kogenluft	*Kommandierender General der Luftstreitkräfte* – commanding general of Army Air Service; post created Oct 1916
Koluft	*Kommandeur der Luftschiffer* – commander of balloon troops at each army HQ
Koluftheim	Commander of Home Air Defence – post created Dec 1916
OHL	*Oberste Heeresleitung* – Army High Command
s	*sächsisches* – suffix to unit number indicating Saxon
Schusta	*Schutzstaffel* – (1916) reconnaissance escort unit; (mid 1917–Mar 1918) infantry support unit
Schlasta	*Schlachtstaffel* – (from Mar 1918) infantry support unit
Stofl	*Stabsoffizier der Flieger* – air unit co-ordination officer at each army HQ; from Oct 1916, Kofl (qv)
56 **w**	*württembergisches* – suffix to unit number indicating Württemberg

THE PLATES

A: SERVICE DRESS, 1914–16

The Air Service was formed within the Communications branch, and consequently retained many of the uniform features of that branch – which itself followed those of the Engineers.[1] The pre-war headgear was a shako similar to that worn by Jäger, Schützen and the See Bataillon. In Flieger Bataillon Nr.1, which was attached to the Guard Corps, the shako bore the Guard star; in the 2nd, 3rd and 4th Bns this was replaced by a conventional brass eagle plate, and in the Saxon detachment (3rd Co, 1st Bn) by that state's star plate. A black plume was worn for parades only. In the field, the shako was protected by a field-grey cover which bore the battalion number on the front in green. Prussian

Lt Max Ritter von Mulzer, who transferred from the cavalry in August 1915. He served with FFA 62, KeK N, KeK B and FFA 32b, scoring ten victories before being killed on 3 August 1916 while testing a new Albatros DI. Here he wears the orange-piped lancer-style uniform of Bavarian Chevauleger Regiment Nr.1. Since second lieutenants wore no rank stars, the gilt winged propeller of the Air Service is the only insignia pinned to his shoulder boards. (IWM Q63119)

units in the field were instructed to return their shakos to store in September 1914, and enlisted ranks received a second field cap in return; however, Air Service personnel permanently stationed in Germany retained their shakos. The M1910 officers' and senior NCOs' field cap (which was sometimes unofficially purchased by junior NCOs) had a field-grey crown, black band, red piping round the crown seam and band edges, and a black leather visor and chin strap. It bore the usual cockades, in Imperial black-white-red on the crown and in state colours on the band (Prussia, black-white-black; Bavaria, light blue-white-light blue; Saxony, green-white-green). The enlisted men's cap was of the same colours but without the visor and chin strap.

In 1st & 2nd Airship Bns and all Flying Bns the black-piped collar of the Prussian officers' red-piped M1910 field tunic bore silver double Guards braids (Litzen) on black velvet patches piped red (see Plate A1). That of the M1909 enlisted ranks' tunic displayed single white braids without backing; all ranks displayed vertical braids on the cuffs, which were piped black at top and bottom edges. The shoulder straps of the enlisted ranks bore piping coloured by battalion – white (1st), poppy-red (2nd), lemon-yellow (3rd) and light blue (4th). Officers' shoulder boards had light grey base underlay and battalion-colour inner underlay; officers who had entered the service in peacetime retained this piping throughout the war. The officers' double-breasted M1903 undress tunic (Litewka) had branch piping on the collar, front edge and turn-back cuffs, and plain buttoned collar patches in light grey, piped in battalion colours. Officers who had transferred from another arm of service wore their original regimental uniforms with the shoulder board distinctions of the 1st Flying Battalion. On shoulder boards and shoulder straps all ranks wore a winged propeller device, in gilt metal for officers and red cloth for enlisted ranks. From February 1914 a light grey oval patch was worn on the upper left sleeve of both tunic and greatcoat, bearing the battalion number in red.

Bavaria's small aviation branch wore similar uniforms differing in detail (see Plate A2). Württemberg, which did not establish its own flying service before the war, first adopted regulations in 1915 with the creation of Flieger Ersatz Abteilung Nr.10. The uniform was that of the Prussian service, but enlisted ranks wore double Litzen; the shoulder straps bore the battalion number '4' in red cloth, and the cockade was black-red-black.

The introduction from **21 September 1915** of the much simplified officers' and enlisted ranks' field tunics saw few changes in the distinctions borne by aviation troops. A new field cap in unchanged branch colours but with a soft field-grey leather visor was introduced for officers and senior NCOs, and the addition of this visor to the field caps of junior NCOs and troops at their own expense was authorized. Officers' shoulder board underlay remained light grey; enlisted ranks' shoulder straps were now light grey piped in battalion colour, with a red propeller device and the battalion number (the piping and number being omitted in Bavarian units). The officers' double and troops' single collar Litzen were simplified and subdued (and omitted for war-raised

---

[1] See MAA 394, *The German Army in World War I (1) 1914–15*; and 407. *... 1915–17*. **57**

A group of fighter pilots, including Boelcke (centre), wearing a typical variety of off-duty uniforms. Boelcke's field tunic seems to be a modified M1910 type, without *Litzen* but retaining black piping at collar and cuff; the latter seem to be of 'Swedish' style. Two men behind Boelcke wear the double-breasted undress *kleiner Rock*, the wartime version of the *Litewka*, with plain buttoned collar patches in the distinctive colour of the original branch or regiment. The NCO pilot (left) appears to wear a wartime version of the Air Service field tunic, with subdued *Litzen* on collar and cuff. Note at far right the plainest type of officer's M1915 *Feldbluse*, with a slightly darker field-grey collar; and the mixture of stiff leather leggings and puttees. (IWM Q63144)

Bavarian units). The Air Service officers' M1915/16 undress tunic – now termed the *kleiner Rock* – was essentially similar to the 1903 *Litewka*.

Many Abteilungen and Staffeln wore on the left sleeve an oval light grey patch now identifying the tactical unit by red chain-stitched letters and numbers; the range was extended in May–June 1916 due to the reorganization of the Air Service and the adoption of the system by Bavarian, Saxon and Württemberg units. Abteilung patches (FFA & FA) displayed an Arabic number; Festungs FA had an ornate 'F' above an Arabic number; and Bavarian units, 'F' without a number. Bomber units showed a Roman Geschwader number (Kagohl staff), or the same above an Arabic Staffel number. Army aircraft parks displayed an ornate 'Fl.P', and the test establishment 'V' over 'Fl.P'.

Despite the relatively dull appearance of the new field uniform, the latitude enjoyed by officers and the large numbers of them now transferring into the Air Service (predominantly cavalrymen) ensured that groups of pilots on their airfields presented a wide range of uniform details. Individuals retained M1910 field tunics (or simplified versions with plain cuffs) alongside the new *Blusen*; and transferred officers wore their original regimental caps and uniforms, sometimes of relatively exotic cut and colours, with the addition of the gilt winged propeller to the shoulder boards.[2]

---

[2] The anachronistic uniforms devised for the 1966 feature film *The Blue Max* were all based on a version of the regimental *Ulanka* of Manfred von Richthofen – see Plate D1.

A1: *Leutnant, Flieger Bataillon Nr.2*; Germany, July 1914

This second lieutenant wears the field-grey peacetime uniform, introduced into the Army in 1910 and extended to the Air Service in October 1912. The mixture of black and red distinctions echoed that of most technical arms of service; note black piping around collar and both top and bottom of cuffs, and the light grey shoulder board underlay of Signals troops beneath the red secondary underlay of this battalion. Officers in the Prussian service armed themselves with the P08 pistol and the 1889 pattern infantry sword.

A2: *Gemeine*, Bavarian *Feldflieger Abteilung Nr.2*; Germany, c.June 1914

This private soldier has been issued standard field equipment and a Karabiner 98 rifle. The single company of Bavarian aviation troops received the same uniform as the Prussians, but originally with the added distinction of a red 'L' on the unpiped shoulder straps, and the bayonet knot (*Troddel*) of a 3rd Company (yellow slide and crown). When the aviation company was detached from its parent battalion in March 1913 the shoulder straps became plain, and the *Troddel* that of a 1st Co (plain white all over); when the company became a battalion in October 1913 the shoulder straps received a red 'F'. This was replaced nine months later by a winged propeller (both the 'F' and the propeller being in gilt for officers); and from February 1914 the red 'F' was worn on an oval light grey left sleeve patch. Bavarian troops displayed double *Litzen* on the collar and cuffs of the peacetime uniform, and had unpiped shoulder straps; they alone continued to wear the shako in the field, and since there was only a single battalion of aviation troops its cover bore no number. Bavarian officers carried an artillery sword instead of the Prussian infantry model.

A3: *Viaefeldwebel* Rudolf Windisch, *Flieger Abteilung 62*; Russia, 1916

The uniform of senior NCOs (Unteroffiziere mit Portepee) was similar to that of the junior ranks, but with the additional distinctions of *Tresse* lace around the collar and cuff edges, and a large uniform button on each side of the collar. The intermediate rank of Unteroffizier wore the lace alone. This Saxon pilot's light grey shoulder straps are piped in the light blue of the 4th Bn, and bear its red number outside the propeller badge.

B & C: FLYING & GROUND CREW WORKING DRESS

All aircrews – particularly those serving in balloons, airships and the high-flying Reihenbildner units – battled constantly against the cold. Early in the war the combination of low airspeeds and relatively low altitudes allowed men to wear little more than their conventional uniforms. However, these heavy wool garments became unsuitable at greater altitudes, and were positively dangerous if they became damp when flying through cloud and later froze. The most common alternative was leather, which afforded some warmth and was less porous. Special clothing for aircraft crews (see Plate B1) was introduced in December 1913, although it was some months before there was sufficient available to equip everyone. Many aircrew combined items of regulation clothing with personal purchases, a tradition that continued throughout the war.

The regulation helmet was made from leather, with heavy

padding around the bottom edge and across the skull made from felt faced with leather. A flap of leather protected the nape of the neck and another served as a visor. Individuals were also allowed to buy their own helmets, the French 'Roold' and the British 'Gamages' patterns being the most popular. The Roold was made from cork faced with thin leather and with metal reinforcements; despite its origins, this type was seen throughout the war, especially at training schools. However, many front line crews, especially fighter pilots, found it too cumbersome, and opted for one of several types of simple unpadded leather helmets instead.

The regulation black leather double-breasted coat and trousers were based on those supplied for transport drivers. Worn under the coat was a long, heavy, field-grey woollen sweater. A woollen scarf was also provided, but this was certainly one opportunity for every man to show his individuality – many private purchases, or gifts from family or admirers, can be seen in photographs. Each man was issued with two pairs of leather gloves, one with a fleece lining for winter, and one without for summer wear. The regulation leather leggings gave some protection against the cold, but ordinary infantry boots were not warm enough. From January 1914, Prussian officers serving as aircrew were permitted to wear ankle boots with puttees when they were in the air, but this concession was not extended to the other states, nor to Prussian NCOs, at that time. Bavarian units adopted ankle boots and puttees for all ranks in November 1915, and the measure was finally extended to all units within the Service in 1916.

Shortages of material made it impossible to maintain the supply of leather clothing. Alternatives in cloth were sought, using fur- or fleece-lined coats **(see Plates B2 and C1)**, heavy cloth coats **(Plate C2)**, or one-piece flying suits **(Plates C3 and E3)**. A further, unofficial source of clothing was captured enemy airmen, who naturally would have no further need for their flying gear **(Plate F1)**.

B1: Pilot, 1914

This man wears the early issue helmet and all-leather flying clothing as prescribed by regulations. The first goggles were issued in December 1913.

B2: *Hauptmann* Oswald Boelcke, *Jagdstaffel 2;* France, 1916

The great ace and fighter leader is wearing another type of coat based on the pattern issued to transport drivers. The original pattern of 1915 was made from leather with a goatskin lining; due to the increasing shortage of leather, from 1916 onwards it was made instead from cloth with a lambswool collar, as here.

B3: Ground crew

The uniform worn by ground crews was based on the pre-war *Drillichanzug*, consisting of jacket and trousers in white canvas used for drill and as working wear around barracks. The low upright collar was replaced by a deeper stand-and-fall pattern, and the jacket was made rather longer, as here. For Prussian ground crew it was dyed black; for Bavarian units, blue. Senior NCOs did not wear collar and cuff braid *(Tresse)* with this uniform, although the button on the side of the collar was worn; their status was otherwise made plain by their visored field cap worn instead of the junior ranks' visorless 'pork pie' *Feldmütze*. Uniform shoulder straps were often but not always worn – here, those of this unit's parent 1st Battalion. For winter wear Prussian units replaced the canvas suit with one made from moleskin; introduced officially in 1915, this was not widely issued until the summer of 1916. The hobnailed soles of regulation marching boots caused damage to the fabric of the aircraft, so in May 1916 (Bavaria, May 1918) the nails were removed from the boots worn by ground crews. The increased wear on the leather soles proved unsustainable due to leather shortages, and in August 1918 the nails were reintroduced.

This man carries a 10kg (22lb) Carbonit high explosive bomb, of the type dropped manually by two-seater crews. The range of bombs produced from 1914 by Sprengstoff AG Carbonit-Schlebusch also included 4.5kg, 20kg & 50kg HE and 5kg & 10kg incendiary. The later forms had 'turnip'-shaped heads with slightly pointed noses.

C1: Aircraft crew, 1915

A number of pilots and observers were photographed wearing this 'poshteen' style of fur coat in preference to official patterns. It gradually fell out of use, replaced by types

Qualification badges, in white metal. The Prussian pilot's badge (far left) shows an impression of a Taube monoplane flying over a landscape. The Bavarian observer's badge (left) differed from the Prussian only in the details of the crown; the central device is black and white with a red border, derived from the conventional German Army map symbol for an army corps.

from sailcloth with a light leather sole, they were first introduced in January 1915 (November 1915 in Bavaria).

C3: Aircraft crew, 1917
The one-piece flying suit was much favoured by (among others) flying instructors, perhaps because they regularly made short flights at low altitude that did not require exceptionally warm clothing. Most flying suits were private purchases, and so could be seen in different colours – not only the tan shown here, but also field-grey or even white. Based on a photograph, this man has for some reason chosen to wear his full dress officer's belt for flying. The helmet is one of many private purchase types seen in use.

D: FIGHTER PILOTS
D1: *Rittmeister* Manfred Freiherr von Richthofen, *Jagdstaffel 11,* 1917
The legendary 'Red Baron' was commissioned into Ulanen Regiment Kaiser Alexander III von Russland (West Preußisches Nr.1), before starting his aviation career in 1915, flying two-seaters with FFA 69 on the Eastern Front. He became a single-seater pilot with Jasta 2 under Boelcke in September 1916, and scored his first recorded victory on the 17th of that month. Early in 1917 he was given command of Jasta 11, and finally, from June 1917, that of JG 1 – his 'Travelling Circus' consisting of Jasta 4, 6, 10 & 11 – which he led until his death in action on 21 April 1918. Here, rather than repeating the many reconstructions of Richthofen in flying clothing, we copy a photograph of him attending a friend's wedding, wearing the field-grey *Galaanzug* ceremonial uniform of his original lancer regiment. The *Ulanka* tunic and tight trousers are piped poppy-red; the shoulder boards have white-on-red underlay, and bear the white piping and cipher of his regiment as well as the gilt winged propeller – the crowded insignia require his captain's stars to be worn side by side. The use of a pouch belt had first obliged lancer officers to wear their medals on the right-hand side of the chest.

D2: *Leutnant* Walter von Bülow-Bothkamp, *Jagdstaffel 36;* France, 1917
The middle of three brothers who all served with the Brunswick Husaren Regiment Nr.17, Walter flew with FFA 22 in France and FFA 300 in the Middle East, before returning to France with Jasta 18. In May 1917, with 27 victories, he took command of Jasta 36. In December 1917 he transferred to Jasta Boelcke, but was shot down in January 1918 over Passchendaele. He is seen here wearing the wartime version of his regimental uniform; note the red/yellow piping at the top of the cap band only. One of three regiments to adopt a death's-head tradition badge, HR 17 commemorated the 'Black Brunswickers' of the Napoleonic Wars; on the field cap the badge was worn between the Imperial and the light blue-and-yellow Brunswick cockades. His tunic is little different from the pre-war undress tunic, the *interim Attila*, but in field-grey. Note the Turkish decoration.

D3: *Hauptmann* Hans-Joachim Buddecke, *Flieger Abteilung 5;* Turkish Front, 1917
Buddecke's aviation career began in 1915, flying Fokker Eindeckers with FFA 23. Transferring to the Balkans, he joined FFA 6; he then returned briefly to France in 1916 to command Jasta 4, before joining FA 5 back in the Middle East. In early 1918 he returned again to France, joining Jasta 30. With 13 victories, he became deputy commander of

Robert Ritter von Greim in a napped corduroy or 'moleskin' flying suit; astonishingly, he also appears to be wearing spurs. Oberleutnant von Greim scored 28 victories, serving with Jasta 34 and JGr 10. He killed himself in June 1945, two months after the bizarre episode in which he was flown into the streets of embattled Berlin by Hanna Reitsch in order to be appointed by Hitler as commander-in-chief of the Luftwaffe in succession to the disgraced Göring. (IWM Q63125)

such as that shown in B2. A field-grey wool balaclava is worn under the helmet.

C2: Non-commissioned aircraft crew, 1916
The all-leather uniform depicted in B1 was discontinued in June 1916, in favour of one of three styles, which varied with the type of unit. All units except those equipped with Fokker monoplanes or Giant R-Types might wear the style shown here. It consisted of an *Überjacke* in field-grey moleskin cloth, worn over the service uniform. The winged propeller badge was sometimes placed on the collar. This jacket could be worn with a pair of moleskin over-trousers and puttees, and this man has chosen a pair of fur-lined over-boots. Made

A group of aircrew pose in front of a B-Type. They all wear cloth flying coats, but the fleece or fur linings differ slightly. Trousers or breeches are worn with either puttees or leather leggings; and the sitting figures show the heavy grey sweater issued with flying clothing.

Jasta 18, but was shot down on 10 March 1918, only two days after joining his new unit. Like many German officers in the Middle East, he is wearing Turkish officer's uniform, in a pattern introduced in 1909. His lambswool *kalpak* headgear bears the badge of the Turkish Aviation Service, and the khaki tunic has a distinctive red collar unique to that arm; however, he retains the shoulder boards from his German uniform. He wears his 'Blue Max' at his collar, while his Iron Cross First Class appears on his left breast between a Turkish War Medal and a Turkish flying badge. When serving in France, Buddecke resumed wearing his German uniform.

E: AIRSHIPS, BALLOONS & HIGH ALTITUDE AIRCRAFT

The basic uniform of airship and balloon troops was similar to that worn by aircraft units. Only the 1st and 2nd Battalions wore *Litzen* on the collar and cuffs, and also the Guard star on their shakos. The Saxon contingent (3rd Co, 2nd Bn) wore Prussian uniform except for Saxon buttons and the Saxon star on their shakos. The Württembergers (4th Co, 4th Bn) did likewise, wearing their own buttons and substituting their state arms on the shako. Airship and balloon troops continued to wear their shakos until November 1917, when they were discontinued for Prussian units due to the shortage of leather; the other states followed suit over the next three months. After the introduction of the 1915 uniform all units wore light grey shoulder straps with red distinctions: 'L' over the parent battalion number, 1–5 (Bavaria, no number). Officers' shoulder boards had the usual light grey underlay, and a gilt 'L' instead of the winged propeller. Airship crews were issued with the same all-leather flying clothing as supplied to their colleagues in aircraft units, again supplemented by a wide range of private items.

Airship crews might also include civilian contract personnel, especially early in the war, when much of the necessary peacetime technical experience lay outside the military. Civilians served as helmsmen, flight engineers or radio operators, and occasionally even as commanders or chief engineers. When a civilian served with uniformed soldiers he wore the uniform of an NCO (if a crew member) or a Feldwebelleutnant (if a commander or chief engineer). When serving with civilian crews they were entitled to wear the cap appropriate to their rank, and a white armband.

In 1915 Prussian balloon observers were issued with a leather jacket and trousers lined with fleece, leather gloves, felt boots and a heavy scarf *(Baschlik)*. Their Bavarian counterparts had to wait until spring 1916 to receive these; in March 1917 the Bavarian authorities tried to halt the supply of leather trousers, but they were persuaded to relent, at the request of the troops in the field, in November of that year.

E1: *Steuermann, Luftschiffer Abteilung Nr.1;* Germany, 1915
A distinction introduced for NCO airship helmsmen and flight engineers in 1911, was black shoulder straps decorated with an officer-style brass 'L' without the battalion number. They also wore a trade badge on the left sleeve, showing a ship's wheel (helmsman, as here) or a ship's propeller (flight engineer), in white embroidery on black with a red inner edging. The posts of helmsman and flight engineer were both divided into three grades (e.g. the former as Untersteuermann, Steuermann and Obersteuermann), the equivalent of Unteroffizier, Sargeant and Vizefeldwebel respectively.

E2: *Leutnant der Reserve* Peter Rieper, *Ballonzug 19;* France, 1917–18
In 1914, Rieper was a Vizewachtmeister with Feldartillerie Regiment Nr.74. In 1915 he transferred to observation balloons, where his artillery training was soon put to good use with Ballonzug 19. He was forced to bail out of his balloon on several occasions, finally, in June 1918, losing his right arm and breaking his leg. Declared unfit for front line service, he served as a commissioned instructor for the remainder of the war. For his dedication to duty he was awarded the 'Blue Max' on 7 July 1918, the only balloon observer to be so honoured. Rieper wears the heavy flying clothing over his conventional artillery uniform. The Paulus parachute was attached to the large hip D-rings of the same basic harness as that used for the Heinicke; it is unclear why the leg and shoulder straps were not visible in the original photo.

E3: R-Type aircraft crew, 1917
The authorities made several attempts to devise a garment suitable for crews flying at high altitude. A flying suit *(Fliegerkombination)* of field-grey whipcord, lined with either kapok or flannel, was recommended for the crews of R-Types in 1916, but a standardized pattern was not introduced until 1917. Electrically-heated flight suits

remained a rarity. The airflow-powered windmill generator was inefficient; the wire cables were unpopular, and many pilots preferred to face the cold rather than compromise their ability to make a quick escape from their machine. Masks were first introduced in 1915, but originally covered only half the face. Many pilots simply used goose grease or something similar to ward off frostbite; others accepted the risks and opted for goggles with an enlarged nose piece. He carries a bulky, lined flying helmet.

F: AIRCREW, 1918
F1: *Hauptmann* Eduard Ritter von Schleich; France, 1918

The Bavarian Ritter von Schleich (Ritter being a title of knighthood) served originally with 11.Infanterie Regiment von der Tann. Transferring to aviation, he served with FFA 2b, then commanded Fliegerschule I until February 1917, when he returned to the front with Schutzstaffel 28. Transferring to single-seaters, he served with Jasta 21 and Jasta 32b before taking command of Jagdgruppe 8. He is wearing here a British Sidcot suit obtained from a captured RFC airman. As soon as they were introduced during 1917 they became very popular with airmen on both sides. Note the harness for the Heinicke parachute; and the Bavarian silver and light blue lace on his otherwise plain collar.

F2: Ground attack aircraft crew; France, 1918

The most unusual feature here is the steel helmet. Schlasta pilots were expected to fly at low altitudes (90 to 150 feet), making them very vulnerable to enemy small arms fire. The parachute harness was often modified to strengthen it, as here, where the narrow leg straps have been replaced with broad canvas bands. Photos show some harness belts reinforced with double lines of metal eyelets for the buckle prongs, or with double leather straps mounted on the webbing.

F3: Pilot, *Jagdstaffel 300*; Palestine, 1918

While some officers serving in the Middle East, like Buddecke, adopted Turkish uniform, others opted for M1916 khaki drill tropical uniforms, with a matching cotton cap with brown visor and chin strap. The first style of tunic had a fly front, turn-back cuffs and four pleated patch pockets; this later style had exposed front buttons, plain cuffs and internal skirt pockets.

G: SUPPORT SERVICES
G1: *Flugmeldedienst,* France, 1917

The men of the Aircraft Reporting Service always formed part of the anti-aircraft organization, and so wore the uniform of the field artillery. In May 1917 they received their own shoulder strap distinction, a plain winged artillery shell in yellow on the red strap; Bavarian units adopted instead the letters 'FLK' in yellow. Pistols were issued as personal weapons. The infantry bayonet was issued to Prussian units in 1917, and to Bavarian units in December of that year. In the same month long marching boots were withdrawn in favour of ankle boots and puttees, and rucksacks were

issued instead of the standard pack. This man holds the handset of the *Armeefernsprecher* telephone system.

G2: Machine gunner of a *Flamga;* France, 1918

Anti-balloon and anti-aircraft troops also wore the uniform of the field artillery. Particular distinctions on the shoulder straps appeared only in March 1916, when a battery number was added. In March 1917, after Flak had become part of the Air Service, a whole range of different shoulder strap devices were issued. Prussian units all bore the yellow winged shell and Bavarian units 'FLK', at the button end. Outside these, appropriate letters identified the unit type: 'K' (lorry-borne), 'M' (quick-firers), 'O' (defended locations), 'W' (towed), 'MG' (machine gun) or 'S' (searchlight). Outside these again, all except Flamga and Searchlight Ersatz troops displayed the appropriate Arabic battery number. From August 1917, however, Flak MG units were ordered to wear infantry uniform, this instruction being extended to those on Home Defence some days later. This man wears his steel helmet, but has removed its lining – this was thought to increase all-round protection because the helmet then covered more of the face and neck, but in fact it actually increased the chance of concussive injuries, since there was nothing inside to cushion impacts.

G3: Meteorologist, Army Weather Service; France, 1916

Most meteorologists were civilian contract personnel, and wore a uniform based on that of Army construction contractors *(Regierungs-baumeister)*, without shoulder straps or collar *Litzen*. Meteorologists were further

Leutnant Kurt Wolff, wearing a captured British brown leather flying coat with an oblique chest pocket and thin beige wool lining, over his regimental uniform of Eisenbahn Regiment Nr.4. Wolff was killed on 15 September 1917 when commander of Jasta 11, with 33 victories to his credit. (IWM Q63158)

The Prussian Navy seaplane pilot's qualification badge, depicting the island of Heligoland on the horizon; and (above) the Navy airship pilot's badge.

H2: *Oberleutnant zur See* Theodor Osterkamp; Flanders, 1918

In 1915 officers serving on shore on the Western Front were authorized a field-grey uniform similar to that of the Army. It displayed the rank on the cuffs in naval style, or else on shoulder boards; the cap had a field-grey crown. Flying clothing followed Army patterns. Theo Osterkamp began his flying career in two-seaters with MFA II and MFA I, and later became the highest scoring naval fighter pilot with 32 victories, serving in MFJ I and commanding MFJ II; he was awarded the 'Blue Max' on 2 September 1918. Later joining the reborn Luftwaffe, in July 1940 GenMaj Osterkamp would nominally command all Luftflotte 2 fighter units in north and north-east France during the Battle of Britain as Jagdfliegerführer 2 (Jafu 2). Here he is wearing the naval version of the Army *Feldbluse*, with the rank displayed on the cuffs instead of shoulder boards.

H3: *Flugobermaat*, Naval Air Service; Flanders, 1916

Ratings serving in the Marinekorps went to war in their navy blue peacetime uniforms. Junior ratings (Matrose, Maat and Obermaat – flying personnel were designated Flugmatrose, Flugmaat and Flugobermaat respectively) wore working dress of a navy blue jumper with the traditional wide sailor's collar, worn over navy blue straight-legged trousers. The sailor's cap had a black silk tally worn with the ends loose. A double-breasted reefer jacket, the *Überzieher*, could be worn over the jumper; this had an open collar and two rows of brass front buttons. Petty officers (Vizefeldwebel, Feldwebel – aircrew were Vizeflugmeister and Flugmeister) wore the same uniform but with a visored cap bearing an unwreathed crown badge. Warrant officers (Deckoffizier – aircrew, Oberflugmeister) wore officers' uniform, with a petty officer's cap. Combined substantive and non-substantive badges were worn on the left arm or, for warrant officers, on shoulder straps: for flying personnel the badge consisted of a red aircraft propeller superimposed on a yellow anchor. Trousers were worn with leggings or puttees.

In late 1914 a grey version of the blue working uniform was introduced, intended for wear with the sailor's cap and wide collar. In 1915 this was replaced by a field-grey uniform based on the Army pattern. Leading rates and above adopted Army-style *Tresse* braid on the collars of the *Feldbluse*, but retained the cornflower-blue collar patch on their *Überzieher* and greatcoat. This Obermaat aircrew observer wears a field-grey version of the double-breasted *Überzieher* over the regulation shirt. The blue collar patch was worn by all ratings; for petty officers it bore one or two lines of white piping. In contrast to the wartime Royal Navy, no attempt was made to conceal the establishment or ship of the wearer, which was lettered on the cap tally.

distinguished by a small badge worn on their collars – 'W' on a 'lightbulb-shaped' balloon. Those in front line weather stations were affiliated to Luftschiffer Bataillon Nr.2, and consequently wore its uniform, with 'L' over '2' on the shoulder straps. Bavaria did not set up its own weather service until November 1917; personnel wore the same uniform as Bavarian airship troops, with 'L' on the shoulder straps.

H: NAVAL PERSONNEL
The normal working dress for naval officers was the navy blue double-breasted *Jacke*, with gold braid cuff rings to indicate rank, worn with navy blue trousers. Sea officers (i.e. those concerned with the navigation or the fighting of a ship) wore an Imperial crown above the rings; other officers – engineers, ordnance and torpedo officers, or doctors – omitted the crown, and wore velvet facings in their branch colours on the collar: black (engineers and ordnance), or bright medium blue (medical). In peacetime a wing collar and bow tie was worn, but this was abandoned in wartime for a soft collar and tie **(see Plate H1)**. The cap was navy blue with a black mohair band (or velvet in the branch colour for non-seamen officers), bearing the Imperial cockade surrounded by a gold embroidered wreath. Straight navy blue trousers were worn.

H1: *Oberleutnant der Matrosenartillerie* Friedrich Christiansen; Zeebrugge, 1917
Christiansen had learned to fly privately before the outbreak of war. He joined the Navy in 1914 as a Bootsmannsmaat, transferred to flying duties, and was so successful that he was commissioned into the naval artillery in 1916. As station commander of Seeflugstation Flandern I from September 1917, he was responsible for improving the general standards of the coastal stations, and for introducing the tactics used by their seaplane flights. In December 1917, officially credited with 13 victories, he became the first naval pilot to receive the 'Blue Max'. He wears the standard *Jacke*, over a shirt with a soft collar and tie.

INDEX

Figures in **bold** refer to illustrations

aces 18, 20–2, 60–1, **D**
see also individual aces by name
aircraft
  AEGs **11**, **26**
  Albatros **7**, **10**, **12**, **13**, 47, **49**
  Fokkers 9, **12**, 16, **17**, **18**, 46, **49**, **50**
  functions 9–10
  'Giant' Zeppelin-Staakens 28
  high-altitude 28, 61–2, **E3**
  production 44–5, 54
  repair shops **47**
  Rumplers 12
  seaplanes 51–2, **52**, **53**, 54
  Taubes **9**
  technical capabilities 54
  types used 9, 14, 25–9
airfields 15, 49–50, **49**, **50**
airships 22–5, **24**, **25**, 51
  uniforms 61, **E1**
Altemeier, Vfw Friedrich 22
ambulances **9**
Amiens, Battle of (1918) 8
anti-aircraft defence 31–42, **31**, **32**, 41, 53, 62,
  G1–2
armament
  aircraft 9, **10**
  anti-aircraft 32–42, **31**, **32**, 41
Army Air Service
  casualties and other statistics 53
  function and tactics 54
  organization and expansion 43–5
  origins 3–5
  units lists 4, 5, 8
Army Air Service: units
  balloon units 29–30
  BAMs 25–6
  BAOs 25–6
  Bavarian 43, 57, **57**, 58, **A2**
  Bogohls 27
  Bostas 27–8
  FAs 7, 10–11, 12
  FA Lbs 12
  FAAs 7, 10–11
  FFAs 5, 10
    FFA 23 9
    FFA 62 **6**
  Flak units 32–42
  Flamgas 41, 62, **G2**
  Fortress Flying Units 42
  Jastas 16–19
    Jasta 1 9
    Jasta 25 **20**, **21**
    Jasta 26 **12**
    Jasta 36 9
  JG 1 **15**, 17
  Kagohls 26–7
  Kastas 26–7
  KeKs **6**, 16–17
  Kestas 42
  Reisenflugzeug Abteilungen 28
  Schlastas 14–15
  Schustas 14
Arras, Battle of (1917) 7

badges, pilots' **19**, **63**

Boelcke, Hptm Oswald **3**, **6**, 16, 20, 21, **58**, 59, **B2**
bombing and bombs 5–6, 22–9, 48, 51, 59, **B3**
Brandenburg, Hptm Ernst 27
Buddecke, Hptm Hans-Joachim 60–1, **D3**
Bülow-Bothkamp, Lt Walter von 60, **D2**

cameras and photography 11–12, 12–13, **27**, **28**
Carganico, Oblt 26
Christiansen, Oblt Friedrich 63, **H1**
close support units 13–16, 62, **F2**
command 43–5
communications 11, 14, 40–1, 62, **G1**

decorations **19**, 20–2, 61, **D**

Eisenlohr, LtzS 21

Feldflugchef post 43
Fieseler, Gerhard **20**
fighter units 16–22, 60–1, **D**
flares, signal pistol **10**
Fokker, Anthony 45
footwear **43**, 59, 60, **B**, **C2**

goggles 59, **B1**
Göring, Oblt Hermann **21**
Greim, Oblt Robert Ritter von **60**
ground crew **12**, **13**, 24, 48, 58–9, **B3**
Grufl post 7

headgear 57–8
  field caps **3**
  ground crew **12**, 59, **B3**
  leather helmets **26**, 58–9, **B1**
  Naval Air Service 63, **H**
  padded helmets **10**, **11**, **26**, **43**, 62, **E3**
  steel helmets 62, **F2**, **G2**
home defence units 42
Höppner, GenLt Ernst von **43**, 44

IDFLIEG staff 44
Immelmann, Lt Max **5**, 6, **6**, 20, 21
interruptor gear 9

Junge, Lt Werner **13**

kites, man-lifting 29
KOFL staff 44
Kogenluft post 7, 42, 44
Köhler, Vfw **13**
Koluftheim post 42

Lieth-Thomsen, Maj Hermann von der 43–4, **45**
lorries **30**
Lörzer, Bruno **21**

Marne, Battle of the (1914) 5
Meteorological Service 49, 62–3, **G3**
Mons, Battle of (1914) 5
Mulzer, Lt Max Ritter von **6**, 21, **57**

Naval Air Service 21, 50–3, **51**, **52**, 63, **H**
night ranging 11
Nivelle Offensive (1917) 7

observation balloons **27**, **28**, 29–31, **29**, **30**, 53
  uniforms 61, **E2**

observers 9, **10**, **27**, 48
Osterkamp, Oblt Theodor 63, **H2**

parachutes and harnesses **15**, 19–20, 61, 62,
  F1–2
Passchendaele, Battle of (1917) 7
photography *see* cameras and photography

quarters **15**, 49–50, **49**

rangefinders **31**, **32**
reconnaissance 9, 10–13
Richthofen, Lothar von **17**
Richthofen, Rtm Manfred ('the Red Baron') **15**,
  16, 17, 22, **45**, 60, **D1**
  aircraft **12**
Rieper, Lt Peter 61, **E2**
Royal Air Force: foundation 28–9

Sachsenburg, Gotthard **15**, 52
St Mihiel, Battle of (1918) 8
Schleich, Eduard Ritter von 62, **F1**
Schröder, Hans 13, 22, 47
searchlight sections 41–2
Siegert, Obstlt 43–4
Somme, Battle of the (1916) 6, 13
Stabsbild Abteilung (Stabia) 13
Strasser, Fregattenkapitän Peter **24**
Student, Lt Kurt **13**
support services 48–9, 62–3, **G**

tactics 14–16, 18–19, 27, 54
Tannenberg, Battle of (1914) 5
telegraph 11
telephones 62, **G1**
Thomsen, Maj Hermann 43–4, **45**
training 46–8, 51, 52

Udet, Lt Ernst **18**
uniforms and clothing items
  Bavarian 57, **57**, 58, **A2**
  Drillichanzug fatigue uniforms **32**
  flying coats **20**, 59–60, **61**, **62**, **B1–2**, **C1**
  flying suits **12**, **15**, **43**, 60, **60**, 61–2, **C3**, **E3**
  greatcoats **3**, **43**
  high-altitude aircraft 61–2, **E3**
  leather jackets 17, 58–9, **B1**
  leggings and puttees 58
  M1910 **5**
  scarves **43**, 59, **B1**
  service dress 57–8, **A**
  Sidcot suits 62, **F1**
  sweaters **61**
  tropical 62, **F3**
  tunics **3**, 57–8, **58**, 60, 62, **A**, **D**, **F3**
  Überjäcke **12**, 60, **C2**

Verdun offensive (1916) 6, 13, 16

weapons, personal 58, 62, **A2**
Wedel, Lt von 18
Weimar, Vfw 20
Windisch, Rudolf 58, **A3**
Wolff, Lt Hans Joachim **19**
Wolff, Lt Kurt **45**, 62

Zeppelins 22–5, **23**, **24**, **25**